ABOUT IDG BOOKS WORLI

Welcome to the world of IDG Books Worldwide.

IDG Books Worldwide, Inc., is a subsidiary of International Data Group, the world's largest publisher of computer-related information and the leading global provider of information services on information technology. IDG was founded more than 30 years ago by Patrick J. McGovern and now employs more than 9,000 people worldwide. IDG publishes more than 290 computer publications in over 75 countries. More than 90 million people read one or more IDG publications each month.

Launched in 1990, IDG Books Worldwide is today the #1 publisher of best-selling computer books in the United States. We are proud to have received eight awards from the Computer Press Association in recognition of editorial excellence and three from Computer Currents' First Annual Readers' Choice Awards. Our best-selling *...For Dummies*® series has more than 50 million copies in print with translations in 31 languages. IDG Books Worldwide, through a joint venture with IDG's Hi-Tech Beijing, became the first U.S. publisher to publish a computer book in the People's Republic of China. In record time, IDG Books Worldwide has become the first choice for millions of readers around the world who want to learn how to better manage their businesses.

Our mission is simple: Every one of our books is designed to bring extra value and skill-building instructions to the reader. Our books are written by experts who understand and care about our readers. The knowledge base of our editorial staff comes from years of experience in publishing, education, and journalism — experience we use to produce books to carry us into the new millennium. In short, we care about books, so we attract the best people. We devote special attention to details such as audience, interior design, use of icons, and illustrations. And because we use an efficient process of authoring, editing, and desktop publishing our books electronically, we can spend more time ensuring superior content and less time on the technicalities of making books.

You can count on our commitment to deliver high-quality books at competitive prices on topics you want to read about. At IDG Books Worldwide, we continue in the IDG tradition of delivering quality for more than 30 years. You'll find no better book on a subject than one from IDG Books Worldwide.

John J. Kilcullen

John Kilcullen
Chairman and CEO
IDG Books Worldwide, Inc.

Eighth Annual
Computer Press
Awards ≳1992

Ninth Annual
Computer Press
Awards ≳1993

Tenth Annual
Computer Press
Awards ≳1994

Eleventh Annual
Computer Press
Awards ≳1995

IDG is the world's leading IT media, research and exposition company. Founded in 1964, IDG had 1997 revenues of $2.05 billion and has more than 9,000 employees worldwide. IDG offers the widest range of media options that reach IT buyers in 75 countries representing 95% of worldwide IT spending. IDG's diverse product and services portfolio spans six key areas including print publishing, online publishing, expositions and conferences, market research, education and training, and global marketing services. More than 90 million people read one or more of IDG's 290 magazines and newspapers, including IDG's leading global brands — Computerworld, PC World, Network World, Macworld and the Channel World family of publications. IDG Books Worldwide is one of the fastest-growing computer book publishers in the world, with more than 700 titles in 36 languages. The "...For Dummies®" series alone has more than 50 million copies in print. IDG offers online users the largest network of technology-specific Web sites around the world through IDG.net (http://www.idg.net), which comprises more than 225 targeted Web sites in 55 countries worldwide. International Data Corporation (IDC) is the world's largest provider of information technology data, analysis and consulting, with research centers in over 41 countries and more than 400 research analysts worldwide. IDG World Expo is a leading producer of more than 168 globally branded conferences and expositions in 35 countries including E3 (Electronic Entertainment Expo), Macworld Expo, ComNet, Windows World Expo, ICE (Internet Commerce Expo), Agenda, DEMO, and Spotlight. IDG's training subsidiary, ExecuTrain, is the world's largest computer training company, with more than 230 locations worldwide and 785 training courses. IDG Marketing Services helps industry-leading IT companies build international brand recognition by developing global integrated marketing programs via IDG's print, online and exposition products worldwide. Further information about the company can be found at www.idg.com.   1/26/00

maranGraphics is a family-run business
located near Toronto, Canada.

At **maranGraphics**, we believe in producing great computer books — one book at a time.

maranGraphics has been producing high-technology products for over 25 years, which enables us to offer the computer book community a unique communication process.

Our computer books use an integrated communication process, which is very different from the approach used in other computer books. Each spread is, in essence, a flow chart — the text and screen shots are totally incorporated into the layout of the spread. Introductory text and helpful tips complete the learning experience.

maranGraphics' approach encourages the left and right sides of the brain to work together — resulting in faster orientation and greater memory retention.

Above all, we are very proud of the handcrafted nature of our books. Our carefully chosen writers are experts in their fields and spend countless hours researching and organizing the content for each topic. Our artists rebuild every screen shot to provide the best clarity possible, making our screen shots the most precise and easiest to read in the industry.

We strive for perfection and believe that the time spent handcrafting each element results in the best computer books money can buy.

Thank you for purchasing this book. We hope you enjoy it!

Sincerely,

Robert Maran
President
maranGraphics
Rob@maran.com
www.maran.com
www.hungryminds.com/visual

Teach Yourself VISUALLY™
Fireworks® 4

by Sue Plumley

Visual™

From
maranGraphics™

&

 IDG BOOKS

IDG Books Worldwide, Inc.
An International Data Group Company
Foster City, CA • Indianapolis • Chicago • New York

Teach Yourself VISUALLY™ Fireworks® 4

Published by
IDG Books Worldwide, Inc.
An International Data Group Company
909 Third Avenue
New York, NY 10022
www.hungryminds.com (IDG Books Worldwide Web site)

Library of Congress Control Number: 00-112322

ISBN: 0-7645-3566-8

Printed in the United States of America

10 9 8 7 6 5 4 3 2 1

1K/SW/QS/QR/IN

Distributed in the United States by IDG Books Worldwide, Inc.

Distributed by CDG Books Canada Inc. for Canada; by Transworld Publishers Limited in the United Kingdom; by IDG Norge Books for Norway; by IDG Sweden Books for Sweden; by IDG Books Australia Publishing Corporation Pty. Ltd. for Australia and New Zealand; by TransQuest Publishers Pte Ltd. for Singapore, Malaysia, Thailand, Indonesia, and Hong Kong; by Gotop Information Inc. for Taiwan; by ICG Muse, Inc. for Japan; by Intersoft for South Africa; by Eyrolles for France; by International Thomson Publishing for Germany, Austria and Switzerland; by Distribuidora Cuspide for Argentina; by LR International for Brazil; by Galileo Libros for Chile; by Ediciones ZETA S.C.R. Ltda. for Peru; by WS Computer Publishing Corporation, Inc., for the Philippines; by Contemporanea de Ediciones for Venezuela; by Express Computer Distributors for the Caribbean and West Indies; by Micronesia Media Distributor, Inc. for Micronesia; by Chips Computadoras S.A. de C.V. for Mexico; by Editorial Norma de Panama S.A. for Panama; by American Bookshops for Finland.

For corporate orders, please call maranGraphics at 800-469-6616.

For general information on IDG Books Worldwide's products and services in the U.S., please call our Consumer Customer Service department at 800-762-2974. For reseller information, including discounts and premium sales, please call our Reseller Customer Service department at 800-434-3422.

For information on where to purchase IDG Books Worldwide's products outside the U.S., please contact our International Sales department at 317-572-3993 or fax 317-572-4002.

For consumer information on foreign language translations, please contact our Customer Service department at 1-800-434-3422, fax 317-572-4002, or e-mail rights@hungryminds.com.

For information on licensing foreign or domestic rights, please phone +1-650-653-7098.

For sales inquiries and special prices for bulk quantities, please contact our Order Services department at 800-434-3422 or write to the address above.

For information on using IDG Books Worldwide's products and services in the classroom or for ordering examination copies, please contact our Educational Sales department at 800-434-2086 or fax 317-572-4005.

For press review copies, author interviews, or other publicity information, please contact our Public Relations department at 650-653-7000 or fax 650-653-7500.

For authorization to photocopy items for corporate, personal, or educational use, please contact Copyright Clearance Center, 222 Rosewood Drive, Danvers, MA 01923, or fax 978-750-4470.

Screen shots displayed in this book are based on pre-released software and are subject to change.

Trademark Acknowledgments

Permissions

maranGraphics

U.S. Corporate Sales	**U.S. Trade Sales**
Contact maranGraphics at (800) 469-6616 or Fax (905) 890-9434.	Contact IDG Books at (800) 434-3422 or (650) 655-3000.

CREDITS

Acquisitions, Editorial, and Media Development

Project Editor
Dana Rhodes Lesh

Acquisitions Editor
Martine Edwards

Product Development Supervisor
Lindsay Sandman

Copy Editor
Tim Borek

Technical Editor
Paul Vachier

Editorial Manager
Rev Mengle

Media Development Manager
Laura Carpenter

Editorial Assistant
Amanda Foxworth

Production

Book Design
maranGraphics™

Project Coordinator
Nancee Reeves

Layout
Joseph Bucki, LeAndra Johnson,
Kristin Pickett, Erin Zeltner

Screen Artists
Craig Dearing, Mark Harris, Jill A. Proll

Illustrators
Ronda David-Burroughs, Steven Schaerer,
Suzana Miokovic

Proofreader
Sally Burton

Indexer
York Production Services, Inc.

Special Help
Maureen Spears

ACKNOWLEDGMENTS

General and Administrative

IDG Books Worldwide, Inc.: John Kilcullen, CEO; Bill Barry, President and COO; John Ball, Executive VP, Operations & Administration; John Harris, CFO

IDG Books Technology Publishing Group: Richard Swadley, Senior Vice President and Publisher; Mary Bednarek, Vice President and Publisher; Walter R. Bruce III, Vice President and Publisher; Joseph Wikert, Vice President and Publisher; Mary C. Corder, Editorial Director; Andy Cummings, Publishing Director, General User Group; Barry Pruett, Publishing Director

IDG Books Manufacturing: Ivor Parker, Vice President, Manufacturing

IDG Books Marketing: John Helmus, Assistant Vice President, Director of Marketing

IDG Books Online Management: Brenda McLaughlin, Executive Vice President, Chief Internet Officer; Gary Millrood, Executive Vice President of Business Development, Sales and Marketing

IDG Books Packaging: Marc J. Mikulich, Vice President, Brand Strategy and Research

IDG Books Production for Branded Press: Debbie Stailey, Production Director

IDG Books Sales: Roland Elgey, Senior Vice President, Sales and Marketing; Michael Violano, Vice President, International Sales and Sub Rights

The publisher would like to give special thanks to Patrick J. McGovern,
without whom this book would not have been possible.

ABOUT THE AUTHOR

Sue Plumley has a B.A. in education and taught in public school before starting her own business, Humble Opinions, in 1988. Humble Opinions is a firm that specializes in computer consulting and training. In the years since she started Humble Opinions, Sue has trained staff and employees of local companies, large corporations, and federal agencies in the use of various applications, including FrontPage and Fireworks. She also offers support for the use of different products. In addition, Sue has taught Internet classes at the College of West Virginia and Glenville College. Finally, Sue has written and contributed to over seventy books about computer software for various publishers, including Hungry Minds (formerly IDG Books), John Wiley and Sons, Que Corporation, and DDC.

AUTHOR'S ACKNOWLEDGMENTS

I'd like to thank everyone at Hungry Minds for their contribution to this project. Thanks to Martine Edwards for her encouragement. Many thanks to Dana Lesh for her perceptive and professional guidance throughout the entire project. Thanks to the tech editor, Paul Vachier, for his suggestions; to the copy editor, Tim Borek, for his valuable advice; and to the graphics people, Ronda David-Burroughs, Craig Dearing, Mark Harris, Jill Proll, Steven Schaerer, and Suzana Miokovic, for their work on the book illustrations and screen shots. Thanks to the Marans for this series design. No author stands alone and, luckily for me, the folks at Hungry Minds are the best to work with!

I dedicate this book to Martine Edwards, an excellent acquisitions editor, who has been wise, supportive, and delightful to work with.

TABLE OF CONTENTS

Chapter 1

Chapter 2

Chapter 3

Chapter 4

WORKING WITH OBJECTS

Chapter 5

WORKING WITH IMAGES

TABLE OF CONTENTS

Chapter 6

APPLY EFFECTS

Chapter 7

CREATE BUTTONS AND NAVIGATION BARS

Chapter 8

CREATE HOTSPOTS AND IMAGE MAPS

Chapter 9

SLICE IMAGES

TABLE OF CONTENTS

Chapter 10

CREATE ROLLOVERS

Chapter 11

CREATE ANIMATIONS

Chapter 12

OPTIMIZE GRAPHICS

Chapter 13

EXPORT OBJECTS AND SLICES

Chapter 14

INTEGRATE FIREWORKS GRAPHICS WITH HTML EDITORS

CHAPTER 1

An Introduction to Fireworks

Are your Web pages plain and boring? This chapter gets you started with Fireworks, which you can use to create and add graphics to your pages to make them more exciting.

THE ELEMENTS OF A WEB PAGE

A Web page is a document on the Web. The document can contain a variety of graphics and text.

Graphics include pictures, fancy text, and photographed images.

FANCY TEXT

You can use fancy text to name the page — for your family, your company, or a product, or simply "Home Page." Fancy text is generally large and stands out from the rest of the text on the page.

IMAGES

Images are photographs or other graphics saved in a format you can use on the computer. You can use a picture of your family, of a product, or just an attractive photograph you like on your Web page.

BUTTONS AND BARS

Web pages can use buttons and navigation bars to connect with other pages on the Web. These connections are called *links.* Clicking a link brings into view either another page within the Web site or a page from a different Web site on the Internet.

ANIMATIONS

Animations are pictures that move on the Web page. Common animations include a bouncing ball or pointing arrow. Animations make the Web page more interesting and lively.

USING FIREWORKS FOR YOUR WEB PAGES

You do not create an actual Web page in Fireworks. You create fancy text, buttons, navigation bars, and animations, and you enhance images. After you create graphics in Fireworks, you then transfer the graphics to another program in which you create Web pages, such as Dreamweaver or FrontPage.

PUBLISH A WEB PAGE

You use your Fireworks graphics in an HTML editor, such as Macromedia Dreamweaver or Microsoft FrontPage. You then use the HTML editor to publish your Web page to the World Wide Web.

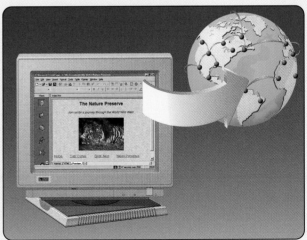

START FIREWORKS

You can start Fireworks to create graphics to use on your Web pages.

START FIREWORKS

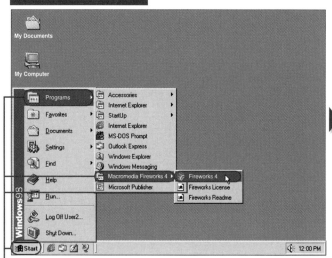

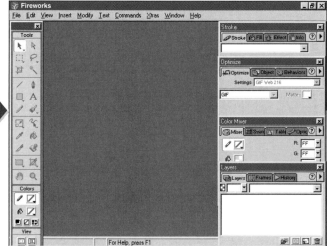

1 Click **Start**.

2 Click **Programs**.

3 Click **Macromedia Fireworks 4**.

4 Click **Fireworks 4**.

Note: To start Fireworks on a Macintosh, open the Macromedia Fireworks folder and double-click the Fireworks icon ( ).

■ The Macromedia Fireworks window appears with the tools you need to begin work.

Note: For information about the Fireworks tools, see "Using Panels."

You can use menu commands, toolbox buttons, and the panels in Fireworks to create graphics for your Web pages.

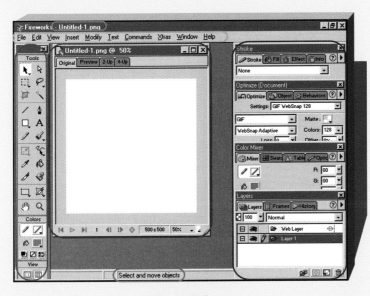

On a PC

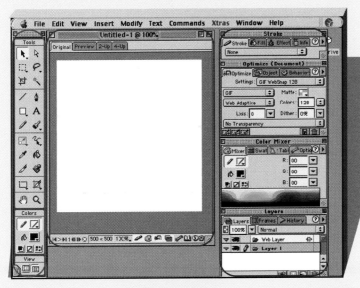

On a Mac

Document Name

Shows the name of the current document.

Document Window

Provides four views of the current document: Original, Preview, 2-Up, and 4-Up (see the section "View Previews").

Menu Bar

Provides access to lists of commands available in Fireworks.

Toolbox

Contains buttons to help you select tools, such as Text, Rectangle, and Apply Fill.

Panels

Provide additional tools you can use, such as styles, color swatches, and effects.

Tool Description

Describes the function of the selected tool button.

USING PANELS

You can use panels to control and manipulate the graphics you draw in Fireworks.

SHOW AND HIDE PANELS

You can show or hide all or some of the panels on the screen by using the Window menu. Just check the panel you want to show or uncheck it to hide it.

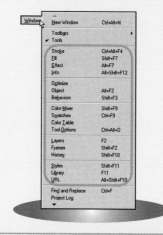

USING MENUS

Most panels contain a menu button (▶) you can click to display helpful commands.

USING POP-UP BOXES

Some panels include a box with additional options. To display the box, double-click an option in the panel.

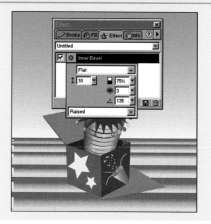

EXAMINE THE STROKE, FILL, EFFECT, AND INFO PANELS

THE STROKE PANEL

The Stroke panel provides various strokes you can apply to lines you draw. You can draw strokes such as pencil, crayon, and watercolor using varying widths and colors.

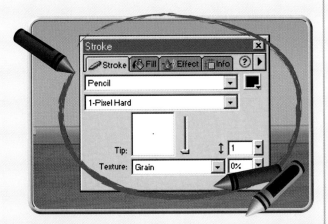

THE FILL PANEL

You can use the Fill panel to apply a color or pattern to the inside of an object, such as a rectangle or circle. You can change the type of fill, the color of the fill, and whether the fill has a texture.

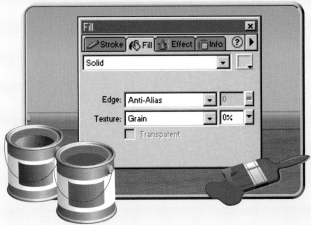

THE EFFECT PANEL

You can use the Effect panel to apply a blur, shadow, or other decoration to the graphic. You can add and remove different effects quickly and easily.

THE INFO PANEL

You can use the Info panel to measure the exact height and width of an object, to locate the object's exact position on the page, and to identify the color palette.

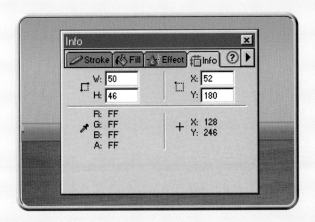

USING PANELS

You can use panels to pick colors for objects. Other panels let you create frames and layers in the Fireworks document.

USING THE MIXER AND SWATCHES PANELS

THE MIXER PANEL

You can use the Mixer panel to create colors and add colors to the Swatches panel. You can also apply colors for stroke and fill from the Mixer panel.

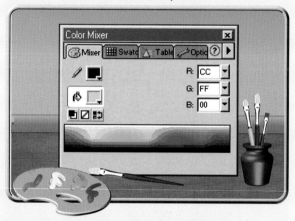

THE SWATCHES PANEL

You can use the Swatches panel to create and store your own color schemes or to access predefined color schemes that work well with Web images.

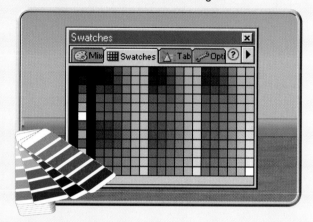

UNDERSTAND LAYERS AND FRAMES

THE LAYERS PANEL

You can add layers to a document so that you can stack one object on top of another. You can use layers to help organize objects in a document or to help create animations and buttons.

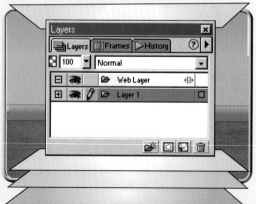

THE FRAMES PANEL

You can use frames to organize objects in a document. You can also use frames for managing animations you create in Fireworks.

USING THE OPTIMIZE AND BEHAVIORS PANELS

THE OPTIMIZE PANEL

The Optimize panel helps you compress images and refine graphics so that they use less space on a Web page. Optimized graphics also work more efficiently on the Web because they take less time to load.

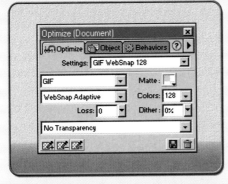

THE BEHAVIORS PANEL

A *behavior* is the action a graphic performs when you click it or run the mouse over it. For example, you can create a button that changes color when you click it. You can use the Behaviors panel to assign actions to your graphics.

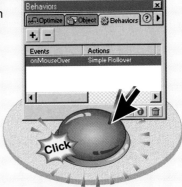

USING THE URL, LIBRARY, AND STYLES PANELS

THE URL PANEL

You can use the URL panel to assign Web addresses to text, images, and graphics. The URL link remains with the object after you export it to an HTML editor.

THE LIBRARY PANEL

The Library panel contains buttons or symbols you create. You can use the Library panel to edit multiple objects at one time.

THE STYLES PANEL

A *style* is a predefined fill, stroke, effect, or text attribute that you can use over and over again in your Fireworks graphics. You can apply the various styles by using the Styles panel.

VIEW PREVIEWS

You can use preview tabs to look at your work in different ways. Each view tells you something different about the graphics.

THE ORIGINAL VIEW TAB

A new document opens in the Original view. You can use the Original view to create graphics, text, and hotspots and to edit images.

THE PREVIEW VIEW TAB

The Preview view tab lets you view
images, text, or graphics as they will
appear in a Web browser. Preview view
also shows you details about the file,
including file size and download time. You
can even play animations in Preview view.

THE 2-UP VIEW

The 2-Up view gives details about the
document in different formats, allowing you
to compare document formats side-by-side.
The first view lists the size of the original
file, and the second view lists the size of
the same file in a common Web page
format, such as GIF or JPEG. The second
view also lists other information, such as
the number of colors used.

THE 4-UP VIEW

With the 4-Up view, you can compare up
to four different versions of your
document. The 4-Up view enables you to
change colors, formats, and other
options to find the smallest file size with
the most acceptable quality for your
image or graphic.

EXAMINE THE PC AND MAC DIFFERENCE

You can use Fireworks on the PC or the Macintosh. The program is the same, except for a few small differences.

KEYBOARD SHORTCUTS

The keyboard shortcuts you use with the PC and the Mac are similar. You must substitute the Macintosh ⌘ key for the PC Ctrl key and the Macintosh option key for the PC Alt key. Throughout the book, when the Macintosh and PC commands are different, the Mac commands are in parentheses, such as "Press Ctrl + Alt + X (⌘ + option + X)."

COLORS

You can use the Windows Colors dialog box on the PC to create custom colors. On the Macintosh, use the Apple Color Picker instead to create custom colors.

REARRANGE TOOLBARS

In Windows, you can show and hide toolbars, undock them, and move them around on the screen. On the Macintosh, you cannot rearrange the toolbars.

FILE FORMATS

You can save graphics in several different file formats. On the PC and the Macintosh, you can save files in the PNG, GIF, JPEG, BMP, and TIFF formats. On the Macintosh, you have the additional option of the PICT file format.

HTML EDITORS

Both the PC and the Mac come with their own text editors that you can use to create and edit HTML. On the PC, you can use Notepad. On the Mac, you can use SimpleText.

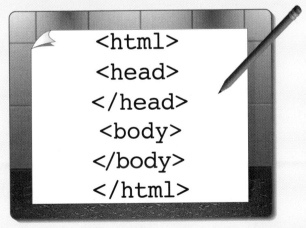

```
<html>
<head>
</head>
<body>
</body>
</html>
```

BIRD WATCHERS HOME PAGE

The page dedicated to people who love to watch birds!

watchers appreciate the beauty and wonder of birds. This month, with summer
around the corner, we will discuss the best spots for bird-watching in the national
of the northern states. These locations have been recommended by visitors to
page. If you have a new location to add, please e-mail us today!

Button

 Membership
Information

Bird

Building a
Better Birdhouse

CHAPTER 2

Working with Fireworks Documents

Are you ready to begin working with Fireworks? This chapter provides you with the basics you need to get started.

CREATE A NEW DOCUMENT

You can create a new
document that holds
text, images, animations,
and other graphics that
you can use on your Web
pages.

CREATE A NEW DOCUMENT

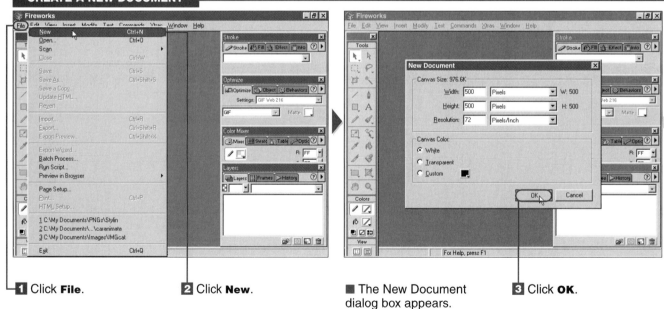

1 Click **File**.

2 Click **New**.

■ The New Document
dialog box appears.

3 Click **OK**.

What file format is the new Fireworks document?

The standard format of a Fireworks document is the Fireworks file format, also called PNG (Portable Network Graphic). The PNG format lets you use a large variety of colors in your Web page designs.

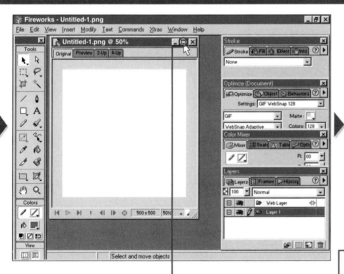

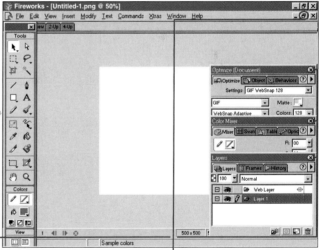

■ The new document appears on the screen.

MAXIMIZE THE DOCUMENT (PC ONLY)

◆1 Click ▣ in the document window to view the entire document.

■ The document window is maximized.

■ You can click ☒ to close one or more of the panels to better view the document.

■ You can click ▣ to change the document window back to the reduced size.

MODIFY CANVAS SIZE

You can change the size
of a document if you
want to work with a
large image or add more
text to the page.

MODIFY CANVAS SIZE

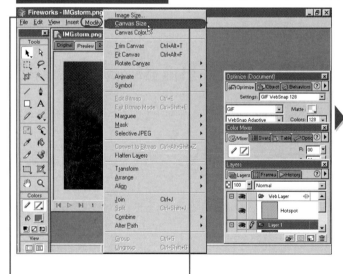

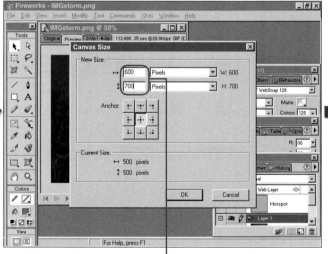

1 Click **Modify**.

2 Click **Canvas Size**.

■ The Canvas Size dialog
box appears.

3 Type a new size in the
width and height boxes.

What is a pixel?

A *pixel* is a tiny square of color that is a part of a larger image. A photograph of fruit, for example, contains thousands of pixels.

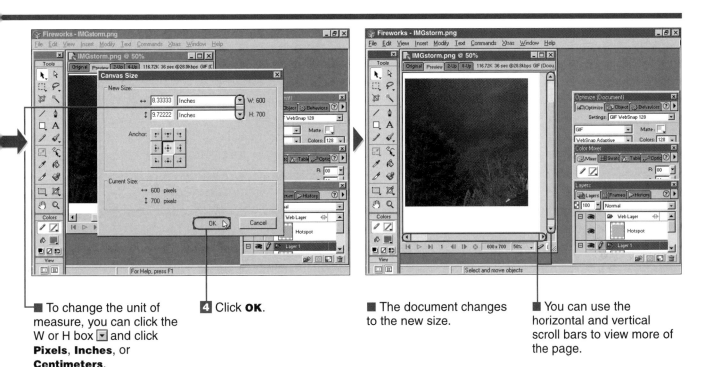

■ To change the unit of measure, you can click the W or H box ⬛ and click **Pixels**, **Inches**, or **Centimeters**.

4 Click **OK**.

■ The document changes to the new size.

■ You can use the horizontal and vertical scroll bars to view more of the page.

CHANGE CANVAS COLOR

You can change the background color of your document from white to any color in the available palette.

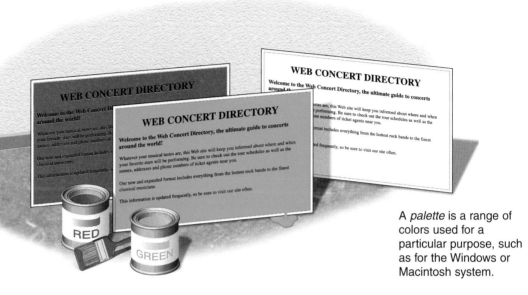

A *palette* is a range of colors used for a particular purpose, such as for the Windows or Macintosh system.

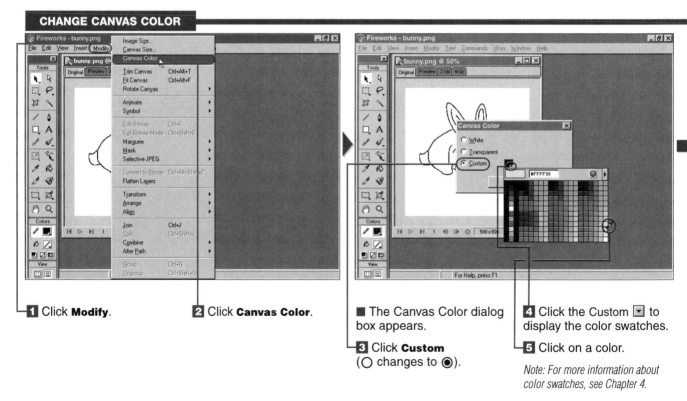

■1 Click **Modify**.

■2 Click **Canvas Color**.

■ The Canvas Color dialog box appears.

■3 Click **Custom** (○ changes to ◉).

■4 Click the Custom ▾ to display the color swatches.

■5 Click on a color.

Note: For more information about color swatches, see Chapter 4.

Why do I need a background color when I am making buttons to use on my Web page?

A background color in Fireworks is not necessary. You can use the background color in Fireworks to match the background color of your Web page, if you want.

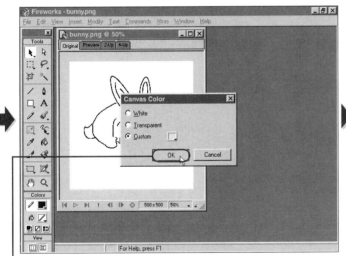

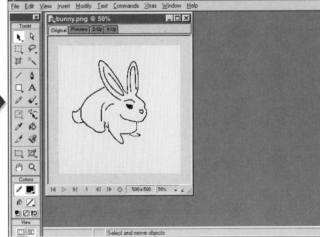

6 Click **OK**.

■ The document changes to the color you selected.

UNDO AND REDO A CHANGE

You can undo most changes you make in Fireworks, such as changing canvas color. You may need to undo a change when the action you took was an accident or a mistake. You can also redo a change after you undo it.

UNDO AND REDO A CHANGE

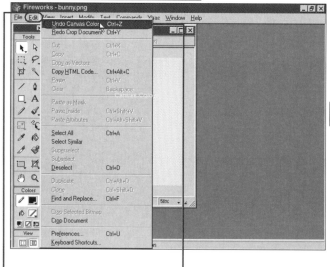

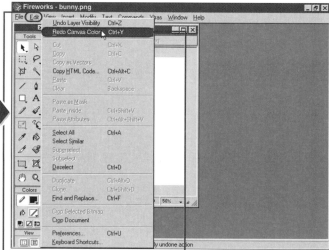

UNDO A CHANGE

1 Click **Edit**.

2 Click **Undo [Action]**, where [Action] is the name of the last action you can undo.

■ The page changes back to its previous state.

REDO A CHANGE

1 Click **Edit**.

2 Click **Redo [Action]**, where [Action] is the name of the last action you undid.

Note: You can only redo an action if you have undone one first.

24

ZOOM IN AND OUT

You can zoom in to view
small objects and more
detail. You can zoom out
to view large objects or
less detail.

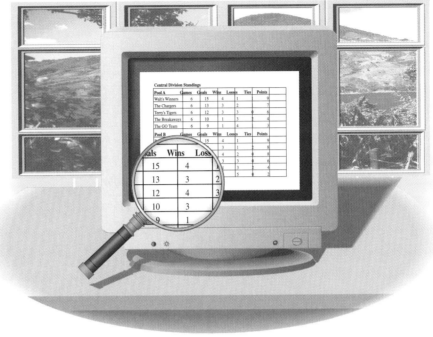

ZOOM IN AND OUT

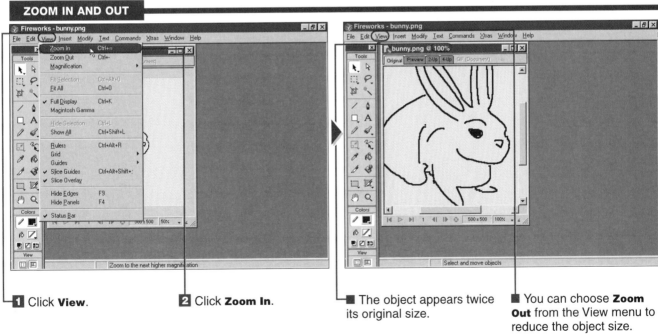

1 Click **View**.

2 Click **Zoom In**.

■ The object appears twice
its original size.

■ You can choose **Zoom
Out** from the View menu to
reduce the object size.

SAVE A DOCUMENT

You should save
your document to
store the page for
future use. This
lets you later edit
and print the
document.

You should
regularly save
your work to
protect yourself
from losing
recent changes.

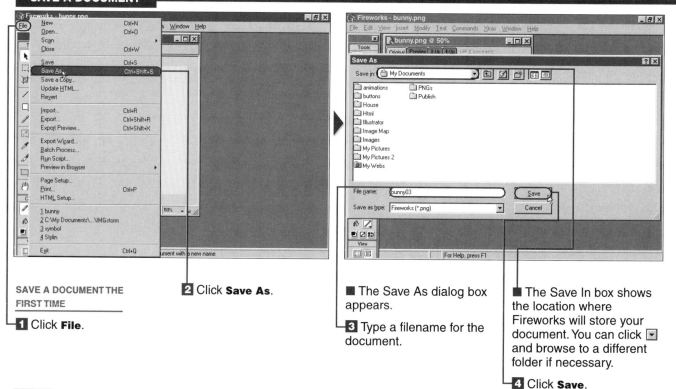

**SAVE A DOCUMENT THE
FIRST TIME**

1 Click **File**.

2 Click **Save As**.

■ The Save As dialog box
appears.

3 Type a filename for the
document.

■ The Save In box shows
the location where
Fireworks will store your
document. You can click ▾
and browse to a different
folder if necessary.

4 Click **Save**.

How can I save a copy of my document?

Start by saving the document and giving it a name. Then choose **Save As** again from the File menu but give the document a different filename. You can even place the copy of the file in a different location on the computer.

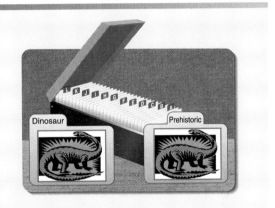

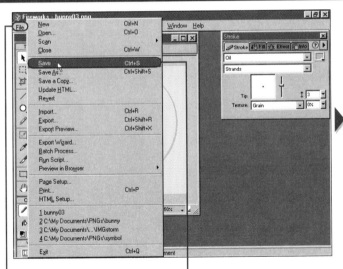

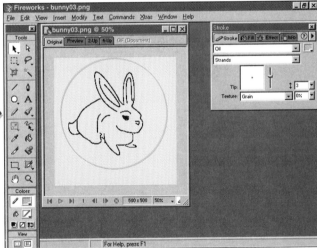

SAVE CHANGES TO A NAMED
DOCUMENT

1 Click **File**.

2 Click **Save**.

■ Fireworks saves your most recent changes to the file you already named.

OPEN AN EXISTING DOCUMENT

You can open a
document you previously
saved so that you can
edit or print the
document.

OPEN AN EXISTING DOCUMENT

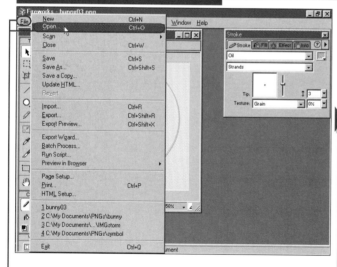

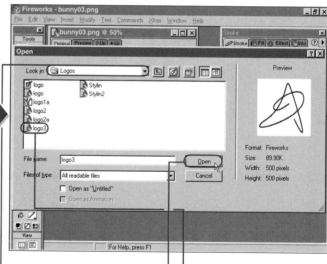

■1 Click **File**.

■2 Click **Open**.

*Note: To open a document, you do
not have to close other documents
that you already have open.*

■ The Open dialog box
appears.

■3 Click ▣ and browse to
the folder that contains the
document that you want to
open.

■4 Click the name of the
document.

■5 Click **Open**.

How many documents can I have open at one time?

You can have five, ten, or more documents open at the same time, but you should close the documents that you are not currently using. When you have multiple documents open, your computer uses more memory and slows down.

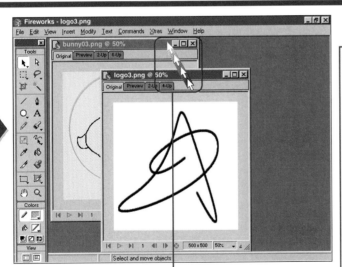

■ The opened document appears on-screen.

MOVE THE DOCUMENT WINDOW

1 Click and drag the title bar of the document window to move it.

WORK IN ANOTHER DOCUMENT WINDOW

1 Click anywhere in the other document window to bring it forward.

PRINT A DOCUMENT

You can print your
Fireworks document so
that you can review or
show your work to
others.

PRINT A DOCUMENT

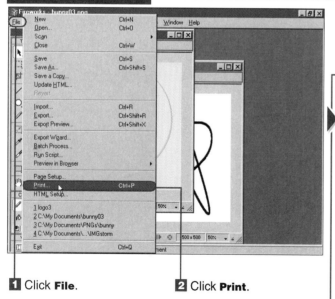

1 Click **File**.

2 Click **Print**.

■ The Print dialog box
appears.

■ You can change the
printer by clicking ▼ and
clicking the name of the
printer that you want to
use.

3 Click **OK** (**Print**).

PREVIEW A DOCUMENT IN A BROWSER

You can preview a
document in your Web
browser to make sure
that it is what you want.

PREVIEW A DOCUMENT IN A BROWSER

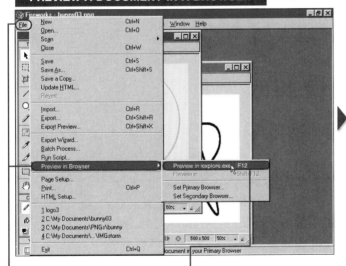

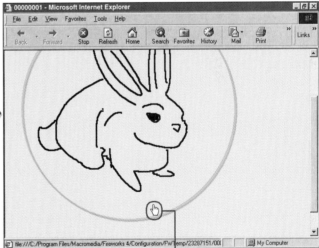

-1 Click **File**.

-2 Click **Preview in Browser**.

3 Click **Preview in [Browser]**, where [Browser] is the name of your primary browser.

■ The text, graphic, or image is displayed in your browser.

■ You can see the mouse pointer change to the hand if the graphic is a hotspot.

Note: For more information about hotspots, see Chapter 8.

31

CLOSE A DOCUMENT

You can close a document when you are finished working with it. Closing the document does not close Fireworks.

CLOSE A DOCUMENT

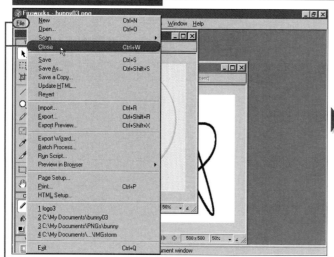

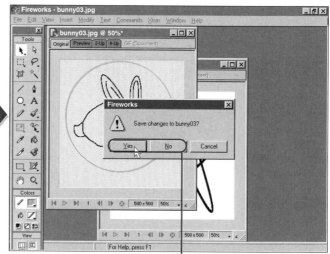

1 Click **File**.

2 Click **Close**.

Note: You should always save your document before you close it (see the section "Save a Document").

■ If you have not saved your document, Fireworks displays a dialog box that asks you if you want to save your changes.

3 Click **Yes** to save the document or **No** if you do not want to save your changes.

■ The document disappears from the screen.

EXIT FIREWORKS

When you finish with
Fireworks, you can exit
the program.

You should always exit
Fireworks before you turn
off your computer.

EXIT FIREWORKS

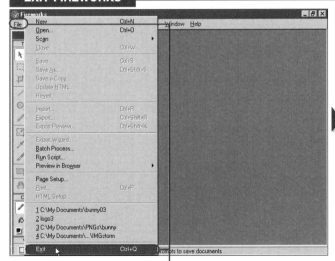

*Note: You should save and close all
open documents before exiting
Fireworks (see the sections "Save a
Document" and "Close a
Document").*

■1 Click **File**.

■2 Click **Exit** (**Quit**).

■ The Fireworks window
disappears from your
screen.

CHAPTER 3

Working with Text

Do you want to create headings and other text that stand out on your Web page? This chapter shows you how.

ENTER AND EDIT TEXT

You can enter text in
Fireworks to use for
headings or logos. You
can also edit the text you
enter.

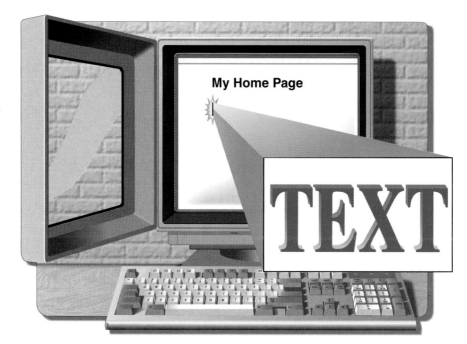

ENTER AND EDIT TEXT

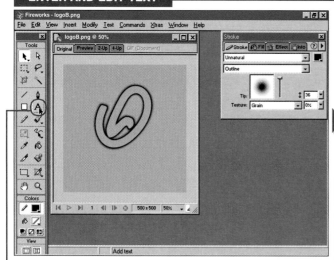

1 Click the Add Text tool
button (▣).

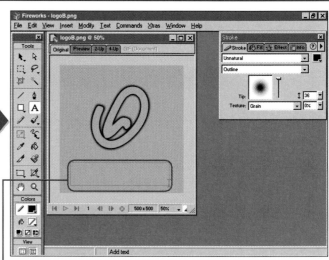

2 Click and drag I on the
document page to draw a
bounding box.

*Note: If you create a bounding box,
text automatically wraps to the next
line.*

Is there a way I can type directly onto the page?

No. You must use the Text Editor to enter and edit all text in Fireworks. You can also use the Text Editor to resize text and otherwise format the text (see the section "Select and Format Text with the Text Editor").

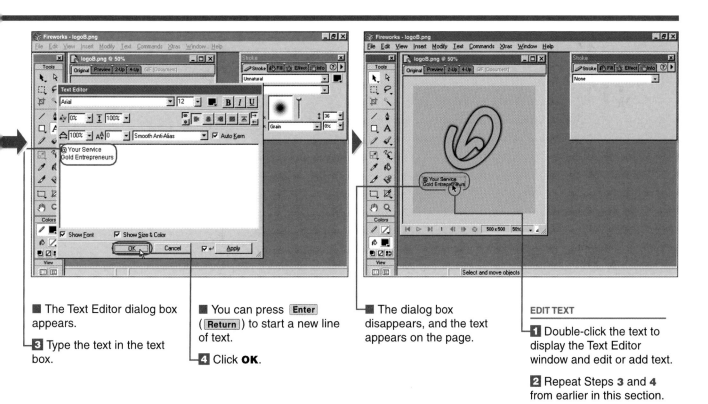

■ The Text Editor dialog box appears.

3 Type the text in the text box.

■ You can press **Enter** (**Return**) to start a new line of text.

4 Click **OK**.

■ The dialog box disappears, and the text appears on the page.

EDIT TEXT

1 Double-click the text to display the Text Editor window and edit or add text.

2 Repeat Steps **3** and **4** from earlier in this section.

SELECT AND FORMAT TEXT WITH THE TEXT EDITOR

You can use the Text Editor to format your text, such as change the text color or font.

Attractions of Bath

Roman Baths
Museum of Costume
Assembly Rooms
Putney Bridge
Royal Crescent
Bath Abbey
Sally Lunn's House

SELECT TEXT

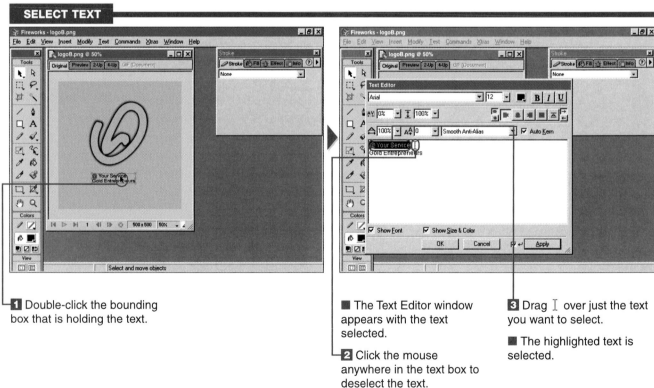

1 Double-click the bounding box that is holding the text.

■ The Text Editor window appears with the text selected.

2 Click the mouse anywhere in the text box to deselect the text.

3 Drag I over just the text you want to select.

■ The highlighted text is selected.

Can I format only one or two lines of the text in a text box?

Yes. Select only the text that you want to format in the Text Editor. You can select other text and format it differently.

CHANGE THE FONT

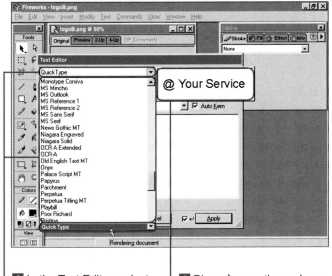

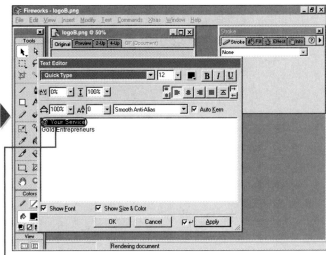

1 In the Text Editor, select the text to change.

2 Click the font ⏷.

■ A list of available fonts appears.

3 Place ⏷ over the various fonts to view each one in the display box.

4 Click the font that you want to use.

■ The text changes to your selected font.

CONTINUED

SELECT AND FORMAT TEXT WITH THE TEXT EDITOR

You can use different fonts and sizes of text to make headings eye-catching.

You should be careful to use fonts and text sizes that are easy to read.

CHANGE THE FONT (CONTINUED)

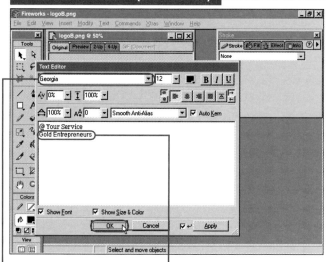

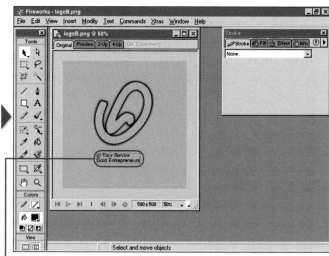

◼ If you do not like the font, you can change it by repeating Steps **2** through **4**.

◼ You can also change the font of other text showing in the Text Editor.

◼ The changed text appears in the Fireworks document.

5 Click **OK**.

40

**How does Fireworks measure the
size of the text?**

Fireworks measures the height of
the text in points. A point is a
traditional typesetting
measurement. There are 72 points
to an inch.

CHANGE THE TYPE SIZE

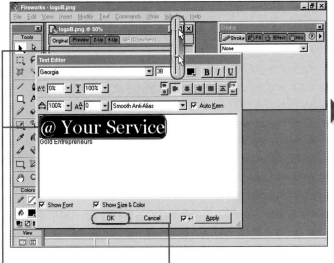

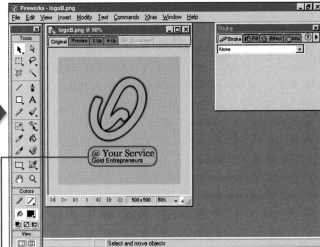

1 In the Text Editor, select
the text.

2 Click ⏷ and drag the slider
to the size that you want.

*Note: You can also select the number
in the Size box and type a new size
value.*

3 Click **OK**.

■ The text appears in the
document at the new size
you selected.

CONTINUED

SELECT AND FORMAT TEXT WITH THE TEXT EDITOR

You can use the Text Editor to change the color of text and text attributes. Attributes are bold, italic, and underline.

CHANGE TEXT COLOR

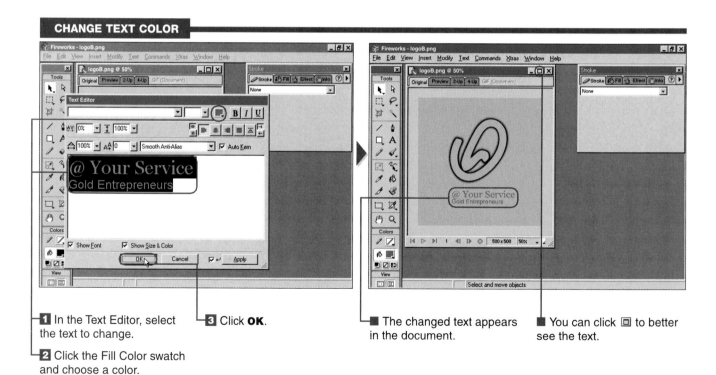

1 In the Text Editor, select the text to change.

2 Click the Fill Color swatch and choose a color.

3 Click **OK**.

■ The changed text appears in the document.

■ You can click ▣ to better see the text.

Are there any colors that are best to use for text on a Web page?

Yes. If you have a dark background on your Web page, use light-colored text. For light backgrounds, use dark text. The most important rule to remember is that the text should be easy to read.

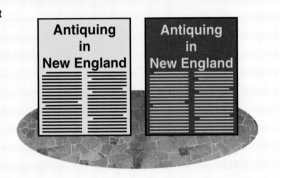

MAKE TEXT BOLD OR ITALIC

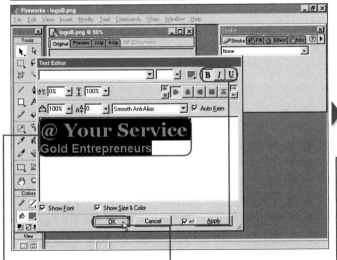

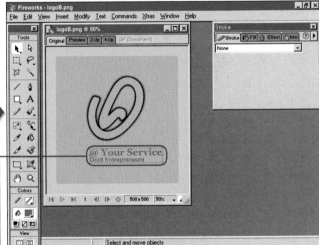

■1 In the Text Editor, select the text to change.

■2 Click **B** to apply bold, *I* for italic, or U for underline.

Note: You can apply one, two, or all three attributes to the text.

■3 Click **OK**.

■ The changed text appears in the document.

CONTINUED

SELECT AND FORMAT TEXT WITH THE TEXT EDITOR

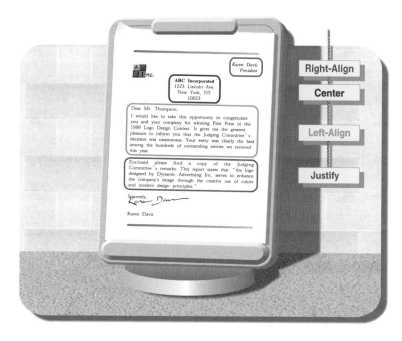

You can set text orientation to vertical or horizontal. You can also set text alignment within a text frame.

Right-Align

Center

Left-Align

Justify

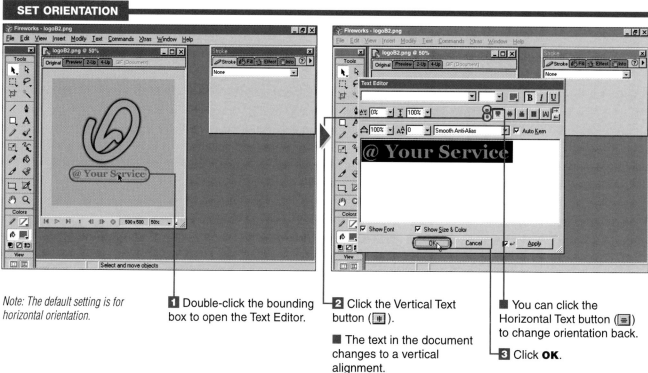

Note: The default setting is for horizontal orientation.

1 Double-click the bounding box to open the Text Editor.

2 Click the Vertical Text button (▥).

■ The text in the document changes to a vertical alignment.

■ You can click the Horizontal Text button (▤) to change orientation back.

3 Click **OK**.

What if I want two lines of text side-by-side with a vertical orientation?

You should put each line of text in a separate bounding box. Because vertical text is difficult to read, make sure that you use only one or two words of text in vertical alignment, such as in logos.

SET ALIGNMENT

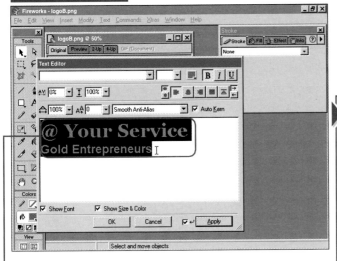

1 In the Text Editor, select the text to change.

Note: You can select one, two, or all lines of text to align in the text box.

2 Click the Left (▤), Center (▤), Right (▤), or Justified Alignment (▤) button.

3 Click **OK**.

Note: Alignment does not show in the Text Editor, but it does show in the document.

MOVE OR COPY TEXT

You can move a text bounding box in the document page so that you can better see it or place it near another graphic. You can also copy text within a document or to another document.

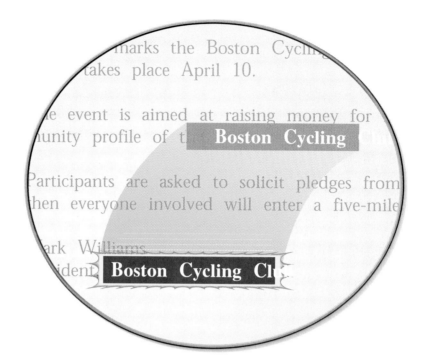

marks the Boston Cycling takes place April 10.

e event is aimed at raising money for unity profile of t   **Boston   Cycling   Clu**

Participants are asked to solicit pledges from hen everyone involved will enter a five-mile

ark Williams ident   **Boston   Cycling   Clu**

MOVE TEXT

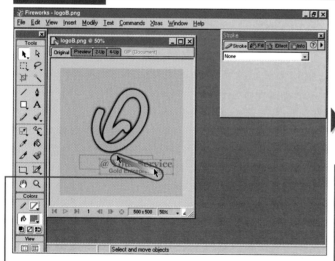

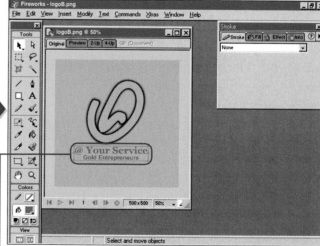

1 Click the bounding box and drag it to the new position.

Note: When you move ▶ over an object, the object becomes outlined in red. Click the object to select it, and the outline turns blue.

■ The text appears in its new location.

What happens if I click and drag one of the small squares on the bounding box?

The six small squares located on the corners and ends of the bounding box are called *handles*. If you click and drag a handle, you can enlarge the text block frame horizontally but not vertically. The text adjusts its alignment within the text block frame, but otherwise, the text does not change.

COPY AND PASTE TEXT

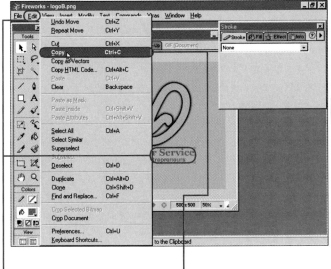

1 Select the text block.

2 Click **Edit**.

3 Click **Copy**.

Note: You can paste the text to another document window by opening or displaying the window before Steps 4 and 5.

4 Click **Edit**.

5 Click **Paste**.

■ The pasted object appears on top of the original.

■ You can move the pasted object down the page to view it.

IMPORT TEXT

You can import text from other programs, such as a word processing program.

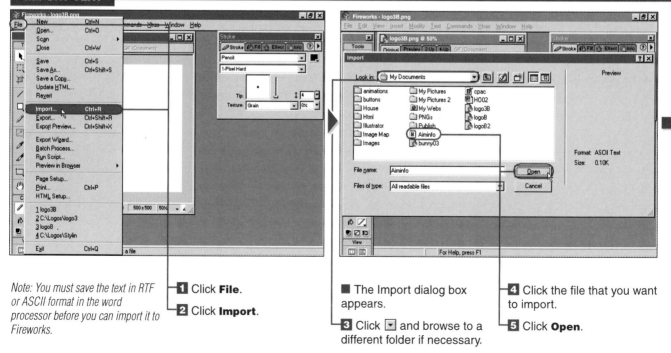

Note: You must save the text in RTF or ASCII format in the word processor before you can import it to Fireworks.

1 Click **File**.

2 Click **Import**.

■ The Import dialog box appears.

3 Click ▣ and browse to a different folder if necessary.

4 Click the file that you want to import.

5 Click **Open**.

My text imported in the wrong font and type size. Why?

Fireworks imports the text to fit a default bounding box in a default text size. You can change the font, text size, and other text characteristics in the Text Editor. Changes you make to the text appear only in Fireworks, not in the original word processing program.

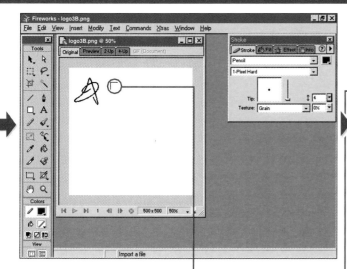

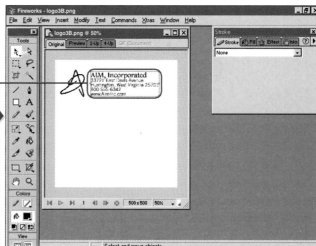

■ The mouse pointer changes to ⌐.

6 Click ⌐ on the document page.

■ The imported text flows into the frame.

Note: You can double-click the text block to change the text size. See "Select and Format Text with the Text Editor."

Note: For information about attaching text to a path, see Chapter 4.

TRANSFORM TEXT

You can transform text by rotating, distorting, and flipping the text to create interesting graphic designs.

ROTATE TEXT

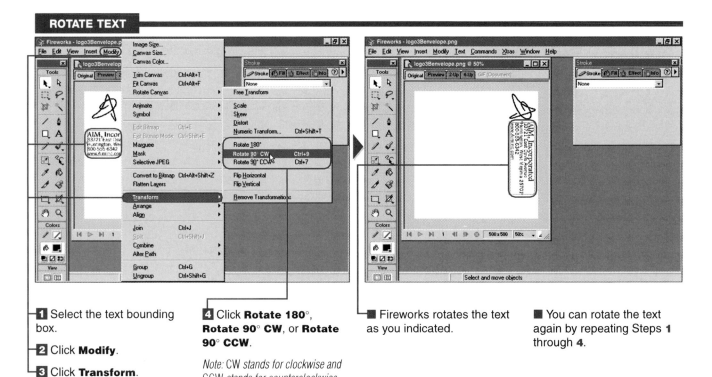

1 Select the text bounding box.

2 Click **Modify**.

3 Click **Transform**.

4 Click **Rotate 180°**, **Rotate 90° CW**, or **Rotate 90° CCW**.

Note: CW *stands for clockwise and* CCW *stands for counterclockwise.*

■ Fireworks rotates the text as you indicated.

■ You can rotate the text again by repeating Steps **1** through **4**.

**Can I add stroke, fill, and effects
to text?**

Yes. However, when you apply a
stroke, a fill, or an effect to text,
the text becomes a graphic, so
the text can no longer be edited
in the Text Editor. See Chapters 4
and 6 for information about stroke,
fill, and effects.

DISTORT TEXT

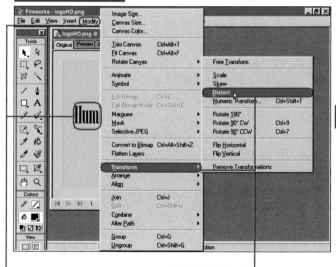

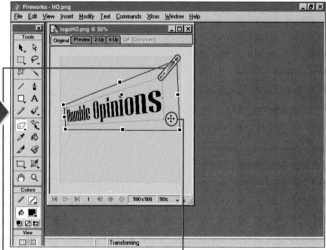

1 Select the text bounding
box.

2 Click **Modify**.

3 Click **Transform**.

4 Click **Distort**.

5 Click and drag a handle to
distort the text.

6 Double-click the
bounding box when you
are finished to return to the
bounding box.

CONTINUED

TRANSFORM TEXT

You can flip text to better suit your design. You can also remove all transformations if your experiments do not work out.

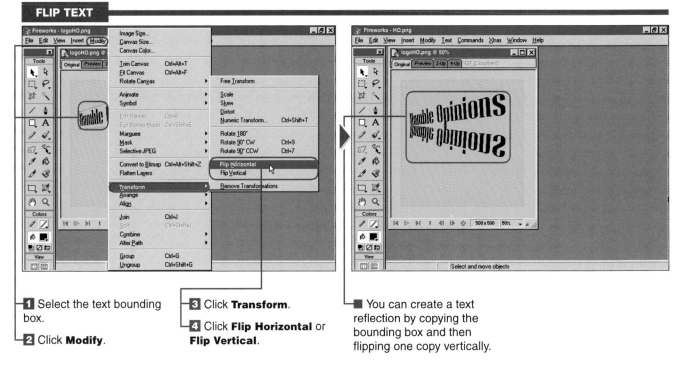

1 Select the text bounding box.

2 Click **Modify**.

3 Click **Transform**.

4 Click **Flip Horizontal** or **Flip Vertical**.

■ You can create a text reflection by copying the bounding box and then flipping one copy vertically.

Why would I flip or otherwise transform text? Wouldn't it be hard to read?

Yes, transformed text is often hard to read, so you should transform only one or two words of text, such as in a logo or a headline. Do not transform a whole sentence or a paragraph of text.

REMOVE ALL TRANSFORMATIONS

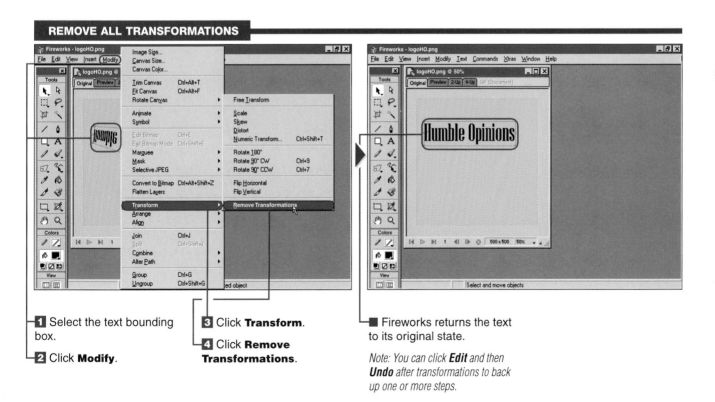

-**1** Select the text bounding box.

-**2** Click **Modify**.

3 Click **Transform**.

-**4** Click **Remove Transformations**.

-■ Fireworks returns the text to its original state.

*Note: You can click **Edit** and then **Undo** after transformations to back up one or more steps.*

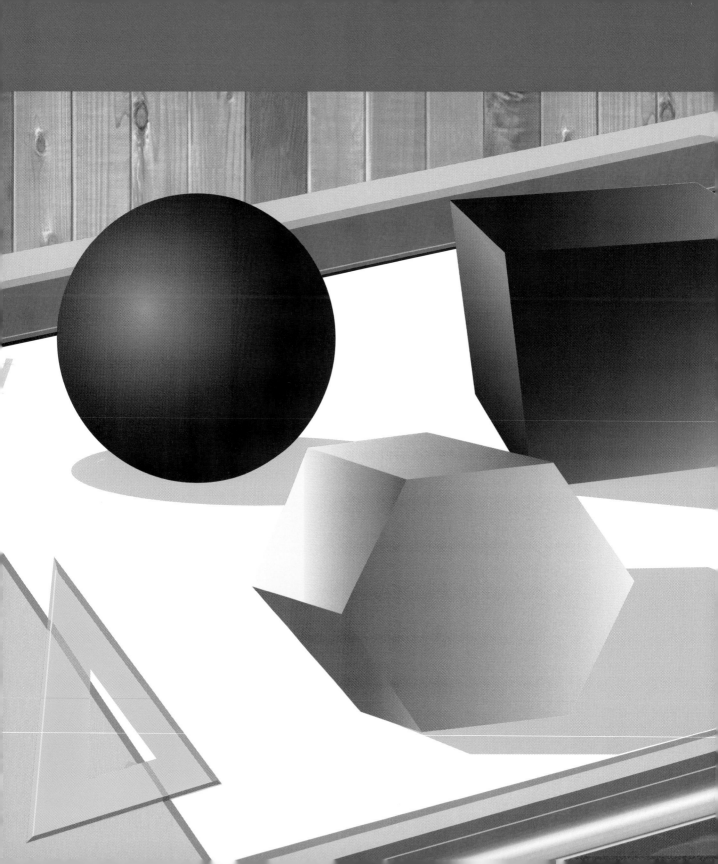

CHAPTER 4

Working with Objects

Do you want to draw lines and shapes to use on your Web pages? This chapter shows you how to draw objects with Fireworks and how to work with those objects.

DRAW LINES

You can draw straight or curved lines. Lines are useful for separating text or objects or for creating drawings.

In Fireworks, lines are also called *paths*.

DRAW A STRAIGHT LINE

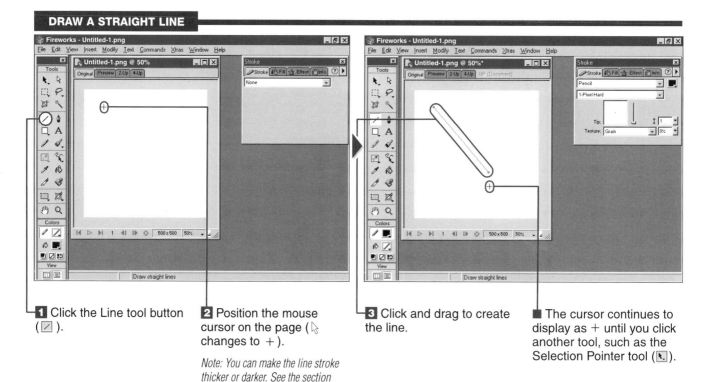

1 Click the Line tool button (⬜).

2 Position the mouse cursor on the page (⬚ changes to +).

Note: You can make the line stroke thicker or darker. See the section "Change the Stroke" in this chapter.

3 Click and drag to create the line.

■ The cursor continues to display as + until you click another tool, such as the Selection Pointer tool (⬚).

How can I create a perfectly horizontal or vertical line?

To create a horizontal, vertical, or 45-degree angled line, hold the `Shift` key as you draw the line, and Fireworks snaps the line into place when you release the mouse button. When you complete drawing the line, release the mouse button and then release the `Shift` key.

DRAW FREEFORM LINES

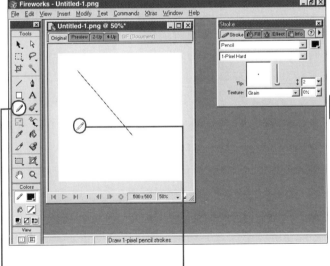

1 Click the Pencil tool button (✐).

Note: The Brush tool (✐) creates similar effects to the Pencil tool.

2 Position the cursor on the page (☐ changes to ✐).

3 Click and drag to create the drawing.

■ The cursor continues to display as ✐ until you click another tool, such as ☐.

CONTINUED ▶

DRAW LINES

Although you can draw freeform lines with the Brush and Pencil tools, you can draw smoother curves with the Pen tool.

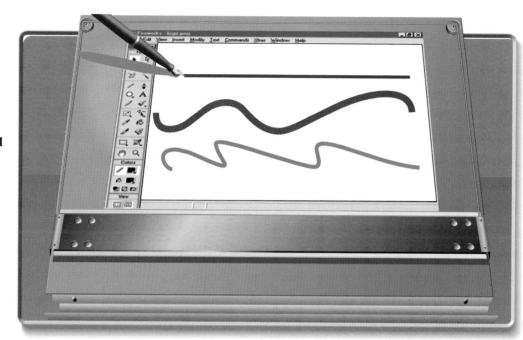

A *Bezier curve* is a smooth curve segment automatically formed between two points.

DRAW BEZIER CURVES

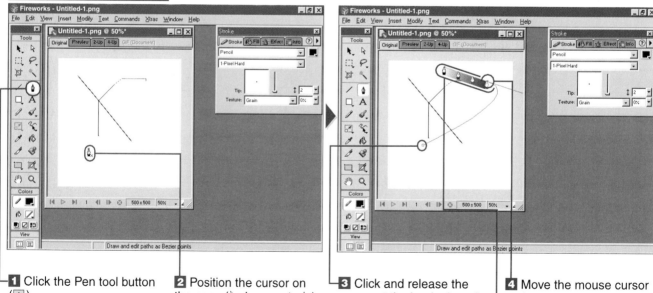

1 Click the Pen tool button (⬙).

2 Position the cursor on the page (⬙ changes to ⬙).

3 Click and release the cursor at the beginning of the curve.

4 Move the mouse cursor to the end of where you want the curve to be.

5 Click and drag the control handle to form the curve.

Can I use the lines I draw to create a shape?

Yes, you can create a shape by moving the Pen, Pencil, or Brush tool over the beginning point of the line. You can then fill the shape like you would any other shape you create. See "Apply a Fill."

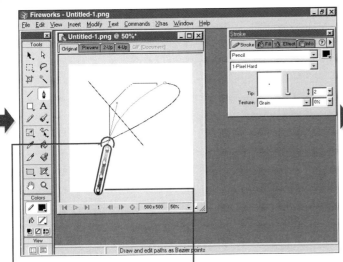

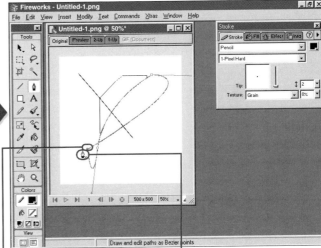

6 Move the mouse cursor to another position to continue the curve or start a new one.

7 Click and drag to adjust the curve.

Note: You can adjust a curve after you draw it. See "Edit a Path."

8 Double-click at the last end point of the line to complete the line.

■ The cursor continues to display as ✍ until you click another tool, such as ▶.

You can change the path
any line takes after you
draw it.

EDIT A PATH

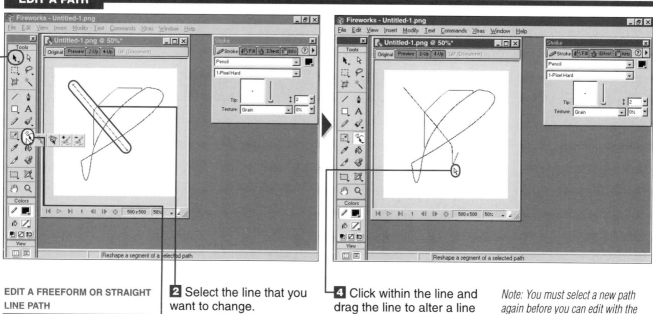

**EDIT A FREEFORM OR STRAIGHT
LINE PATH**

1 Click the Selection
Pointer tool ().

2 Select the line that you
want to change.

3 Click the Freeform tool
(■).

4 Click within the line and
drag the line to alter a line
segment.

*Note: You must select a new path
again before you can edit with the
Freeform tool.*

Can I use the Freeform tool on a Bezier curve?

Yes, you can, but you will loose the smooth rounded curves if you use the Freeform tool on a Bezier curve.

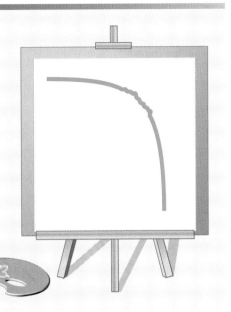

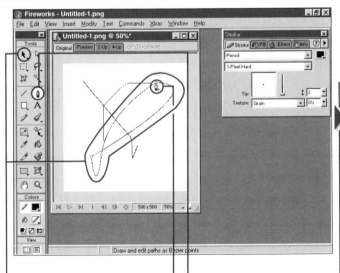

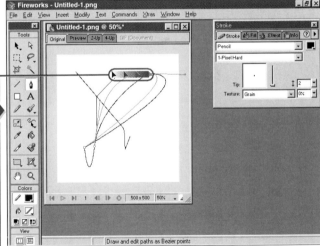

EDIT A BEZIER CURVE

1 Click .

2 Select the curve that you want to change.

3 Click .

■ Handles appear on the curve.

4 Position the tool over a handle until you see a carat beside the Pen cursor ( ).

5 Click and drag the tool to change the curve of the line.

Note: If the cursor shows an X instead of a carat ( ), it draws another curve instead of editing the path.

ATTACH TEXT TO A PATH

You can draw a curve or
other path and attach
text to that path.

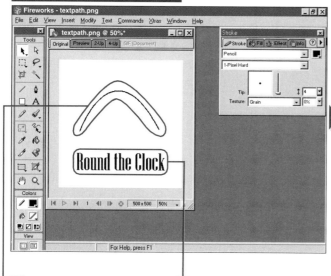

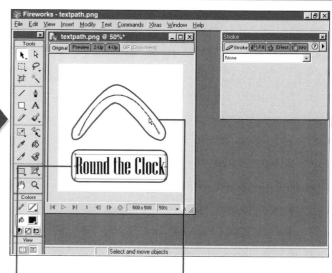

1 Draw a path using ✏, ✏ , or ✏ .

2 Add the text and format it to the size and font you want.

Note: For information about adding and formatting text, see Chapter 3.

3 Select the text.

4 Press and hold the
Shift key.

5 Select the path.

**How can I make the
text appear at the end
of the path instead of
the beginning?**

The text attaches to
the beginning of the
path when the text is
left-aligned. If you
right-align the text, it
attaches at the end
of the path. Center-
align the text to attach
it to the middle of
the path.

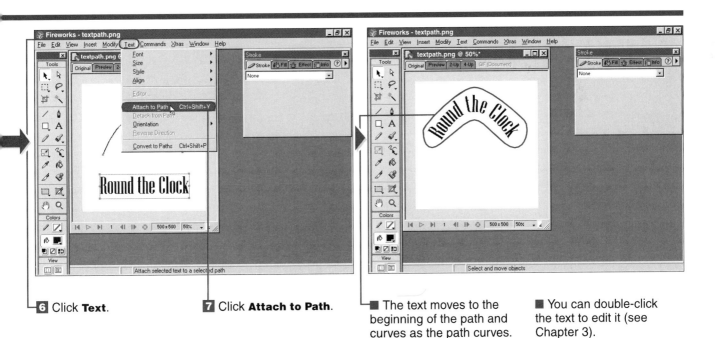

6 Click **Text**.

7 Click **Attach to Path**.

■ The text moves to the
beginning of the path and
curves as the path curves.

■ You can double-click
the text to edit it (see
Chapter 3).

CHANGE THE STROKE

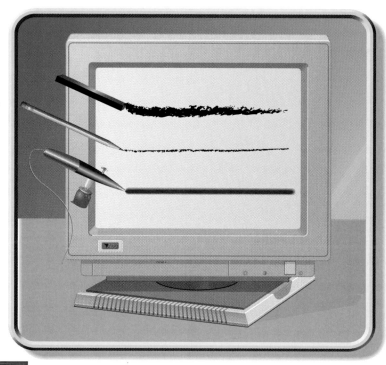

You can change the stroke to give a line a different look, such as a pencil, an air brush, or charcoal.

You can also change the stroke of the line around a shape.

CHANGE THE STROKE

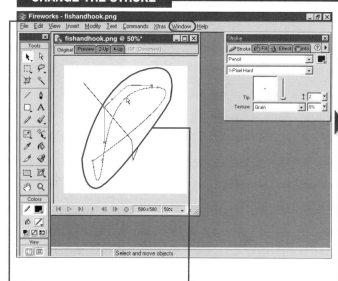

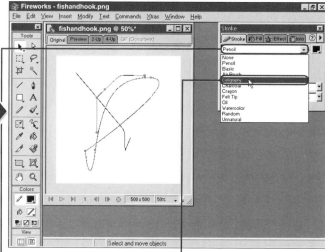

1 Click **Window** and then **Stroke** to display the Stroke panel.

2 Select the line or lines you want to change.

Note: You could choose the Stroke category and other options before you draw the line.

3 Click the Stroke category ▾.

4 Click the stroke you want.

What kind of textures can I apply to a line?

You can use the textures listed in the Stroke category list, such as Pencil, Air Brush, and Crayon. You can also apply paint splatters, toothpaste, and other Unnatural strokes from the Stroke panel.

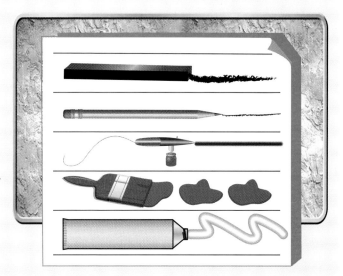

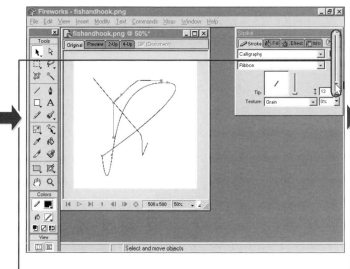

5 Click and drag the slider to indicate the size of the tip for the new stroke.

■ You can click the color swatch to change the color of the stroke.

6 Click the Stroke name ▼ to choose a variation of the Stroke category.

DRAW A SHAPE

You can draw shapes to use in your Web designs, such as a button or a bar.

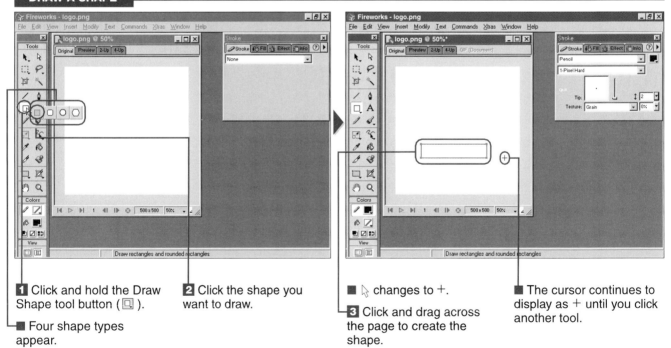

1 Click and hold the Draw Shape tool button (⬚).

■ Four shape types appear.

2 Click the shape you want to draw.

■ ⬚ changes to +.

3 Click and drag across the page to create the shape.

■ The cursor continues to display as + until you click another tool.

How does Fireworks choose the stroke for the shapes I draw?

The stroke you use to draw a shape is the default stroke — pencil. If you change the stroke, Fireworks uses that stroke for all objects you draw until you change the stroke again. Fills work the same way. Fireworks uses no fill until you change the fill for an object.

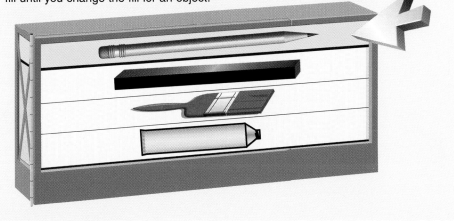

DRAW A PERFECT SQUARE OR CIRCLE

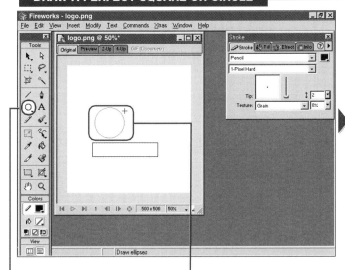

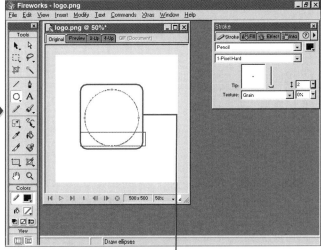

1 Click and hold ▦ and, from the box that appears, select the Draw Rectangle tool (▭) for a square or the Draw Ellipse tool (○) for a circle.

2 Press and hold down the **Shift** key as you draw the square or circle.

3 Release the mouse button and the **Shift** key.

■ The result is a perfect square or circle.

APPLY A FILL

You can fill a shape
with color or
pattern such as
tweed.

APPLY A FILL

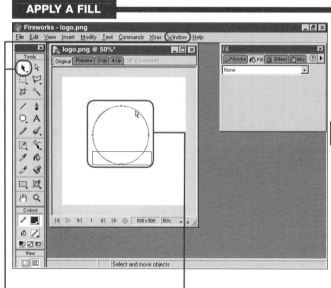

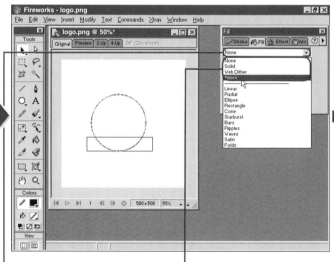

APPLY A COLOR OR PATTERN

1 Click **Window** and then
Fill to display the Fill panel.

2 Click 🔍.

3 Select the shape.

*Note: You can select multiple shapes
to apply fill to by holding the* **Shift**
key as you click each shape.

4 Click the Fill category ▾.

5 Choose a category.

*Note: Solid lets you choose a color.
Pattern lets you choose a pattern.*

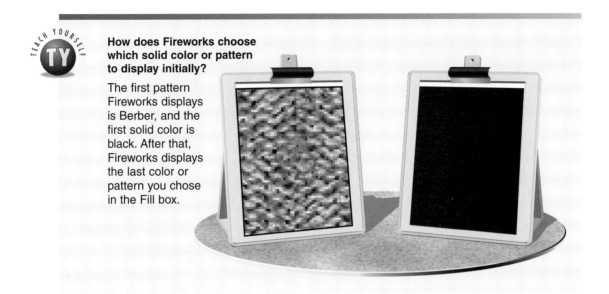

**How does Fireworks choose
which solid color or pattern
to display initially?**

The first pattern
Fireworks displays
is Berber, and the
first solid color is
black. After that,
Fireworks displays
the last color or
pattern you chose
in the Fill box.

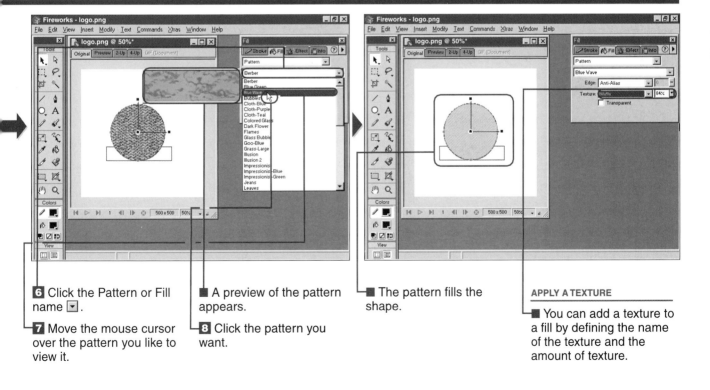

6 Click the Pattern or Fill
name ▼.

7 Move the mouse cursor
over the pattern you like to
view it.

■ A preview of the pattern
appears.

8 Click the pattern you
want.

■ The pattern fills the
shape.

APPLY A TEXTURE

■ You can add a texture to
a fill by defining the name
of the texture and the
amount of texture.

WORK WITH COLOR

You can add colors to your graphics that will look good in any browser.

Use Web-safe colors for the best results.

OPEN A PALETTE IN THE SWATCHES PANEL

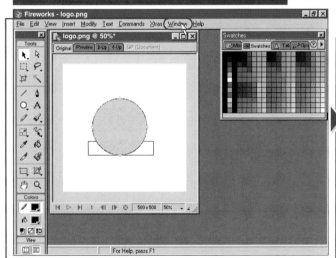

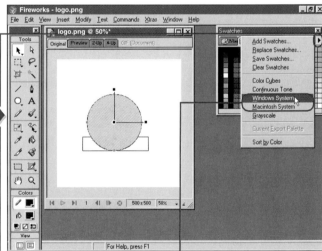

1 Click **Window** and then **Swatches** to display the Swatches panel.

Note: You can hide or display the other panels.

2 Click the Swatches panel Options pop-up button (▶).

3 Click **Windows System** or **Macintosh System**.

■ Colors common to Windows or the Macintosh appear.

What are Web-safe colors?

Web-safe colors are colors that are common to both the PC and Macintosh and to each of the major browsers on those systems. It is a good idea to design your Web graphics with Web-safe colors.

SORT THE COLORS IN THE SWATCHES PANEL

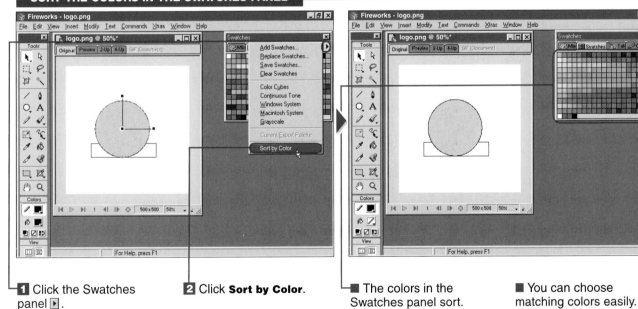

1 Click the Swatches panel ▶.

2 Click **Sort by Color**.

■ The colors in the Swatches panel sort.

■ You can choose matching colors easily.

CONTINUED

WORK WITH COLOR

You can use colors that are not in the swatches, such as a special logo color.

Some colors you pick may not look the same in all browsers.

MIX A COLOR

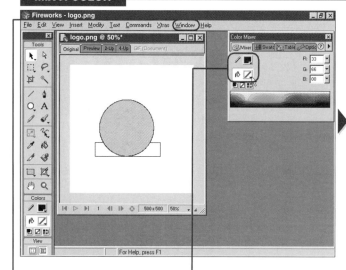

1 Click **Window** and then **Color Mixer** to display the Mixer panel.

2 Click either the Stroke or Fill Color Well.

■ ⟨ changes to ✐.

3 Click a color.

■ The stroke or fill color changes to that color.

What if I made changes to the stroke and fill but want to change them back to their original colors?

Click the Default Colors button (■) in the Mixer panel. The colors change back. You cannot undo this step.

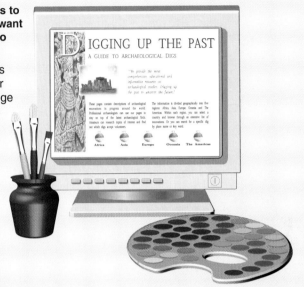

ADD A COLOR TO THE SWATCHES PANEL

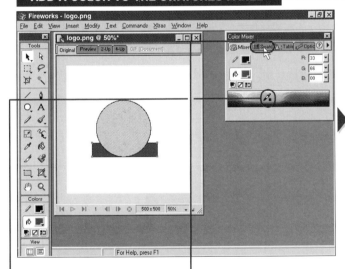

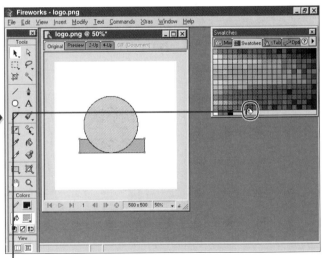

1 In the Mixer panel, click ✐ on the color you want to add.

2 Click the **Swatches** tab.

Note: The color will also replace either the stroke or fill color.

3 Move the mouse cursor to the bottom of the Swatches panel (✐ changes to ⬧) and click.

■ The new color appears in the Swatches panel.

TRANSFORM AN OBJECT

Just as with text, you can transform objects, such as lines and shapes.

Transform an object by scaling, flipping, or rotating it.

SCALE AN OBJECT

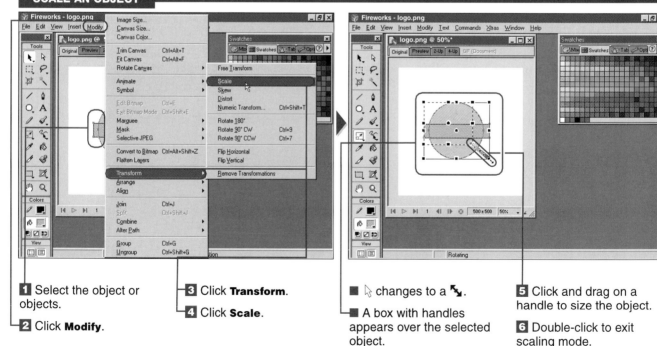

1 Select the object or objects.

2 Click **Modify**.

3 Click **Transform**.

4 Click **Scale**.

■ ⌖ changes to a ⬉.

■ A box with handles appears over the selected object.

5 Click and drag on a handle to size the object.

6 Double-click to exit scaling mode.

■ The size of the object changes.

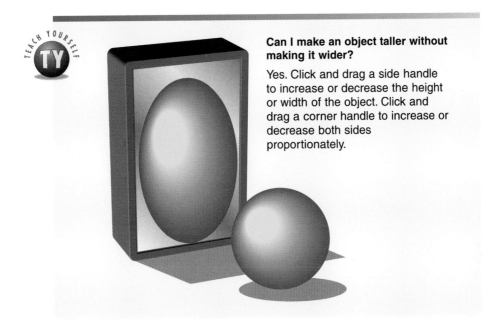

Can I make an object taller without making it wider?

Yes. Click and drag a side handle to increase or decrease the height or width of the object. Click and drag a corner handle to increase or decrease both sides proportionally.

ROTATE AN OBJECT

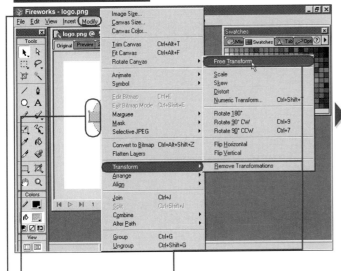

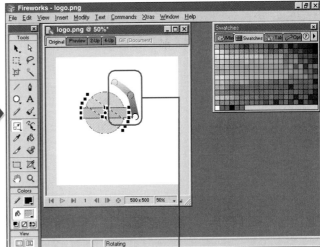

1 Select the object.

2 Click **Modify**.

3 Click **Transform**.

4 Click **Free Transform**.

■ ⏱ changes to ↻.

■ A box with handles appears over the selected object.

5 Click and drag to rotate the object.

6 Double-click to exit transforming mode.

■ The selected object appears in the rotated position.

CONTINUED ▶

TRANSFORM AN OBJECT

You can flip an object horizontally or vertically. You can also distort an object.

You can transform any object in Fireworks, even images.

FLIP AN OBJECT

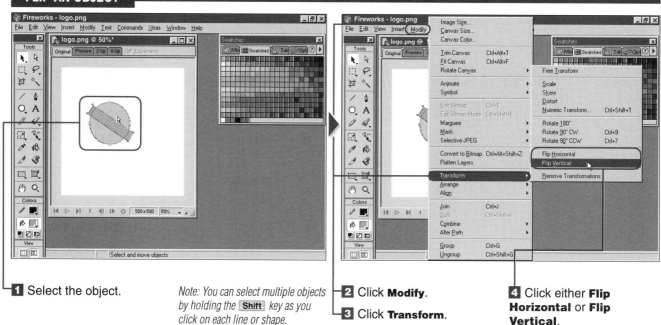

1 Select the object.

Note: You can select multiple objects by holding the **Shift** *key as you click on each line or shape.*

2 Click **Modify**.

3 Click **Transform**.

4 Click either **Flip Horizontal** or **Flip Vertical**.

■ The object flips in the direction you choose.

What is the difference between Scale, Skew, and Distort?

You can use all three to distort an object. Use Scale to make the object larger or smaller only by height or width. Use Skew to stretch or move one side of the object while the other side remains stationary. Use Distort to stretch or condense any side or corner of the object.

DISTORT AN OBJECT

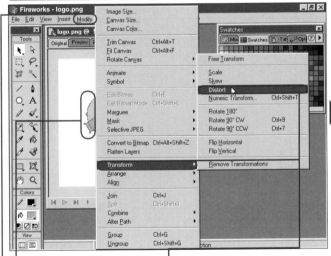

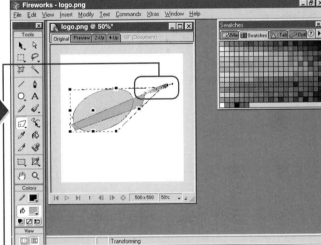

1 Select the object.

2 Click **Modify**.

3 Click **Transform**.

4 Click **Distort**.

■ ⃕ changes to ⤢ for distorting.

5 Click and drag any handle to distort the object.

Note: Use the Skew command to distort just one side of the object.

6 Double-click to exit transforming mode.

■ The object is distorted.

ARRANGE OBJECTS

You can arrange objects in layers on the page so that some objects are on top of others.

Arranging objects gives the design depth.

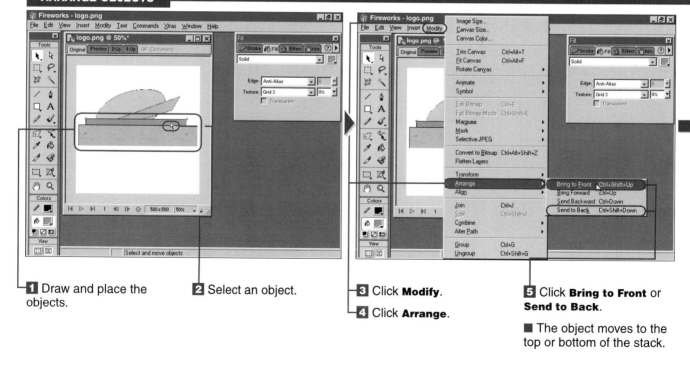

1 Draw and place the objects.

2 Select an object.

3 Click **Modify**.

4 Click **Arrange**.

5 Click **Bring to Front** or **Send to Back**.

■ The object moves to the top or bottom of the stack.

Can I arrange multiple objects at one time?

Yes, you can select multiple objects and bring them all forward or send them all back. The selected objects remain in their original stacking order.

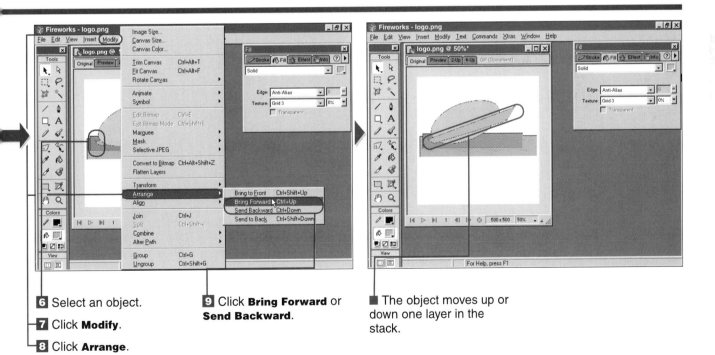

6 Select an object.

7 Click **Modify**.

8 Click **Arrange**.

9 Click **Bring Forward** or **Send Backward**.

■ The object moves up or down one layer in the stack.

GROUP OBJECTS

You can group objects to
apply one stroke or fill to
multiple objects at once.

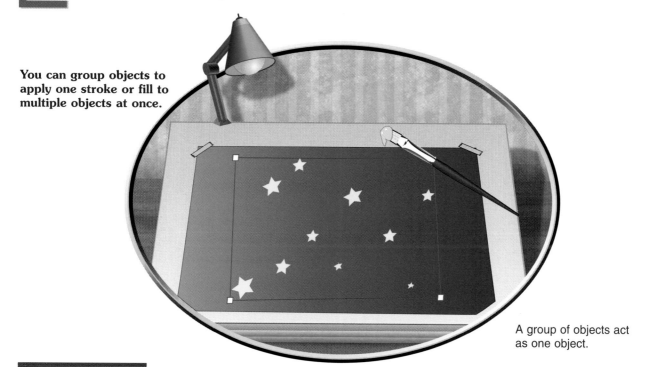

A group of objects act
as one object.

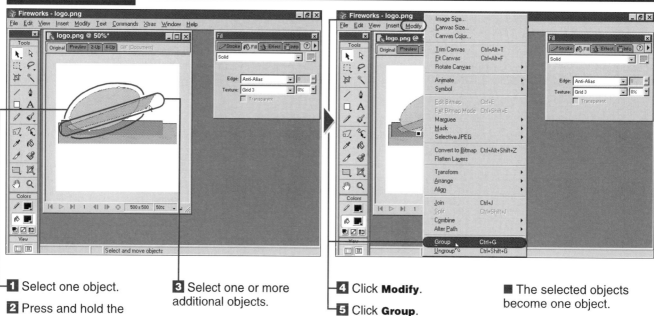

1 Select one object.

2 Press and hold the
Shift key.

3 Select one or more
additional objects.

4 Click **Modify**.

5 Click **Group**.

■ The selected objects
become one object.

Why would I want to ungroup an object?

You ungroup an object when you want to edit or format one of the objects within the group. You can always group the selected objects again later.

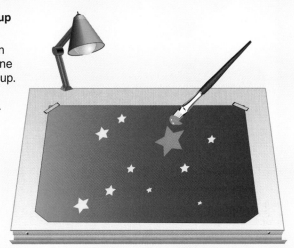

UNGROUP OBJECTS

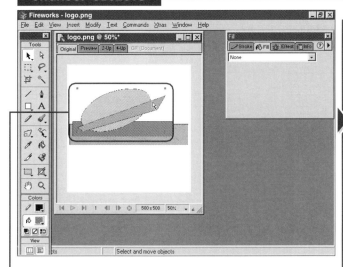

1 Select the grouped object.

Note: Any live effects you applied to the group are lost when you ungroup.

2 Click **Modify**.

3 Click **Ungroup**.

■ The objects are ungrouped.

4 Click off of the selected objects to deselect all.

USING LAYERS

Layers let you separate your design so that you can work on parts of it individually.

You can hide layers as you work and show them again when necessary.

USING LAYERS

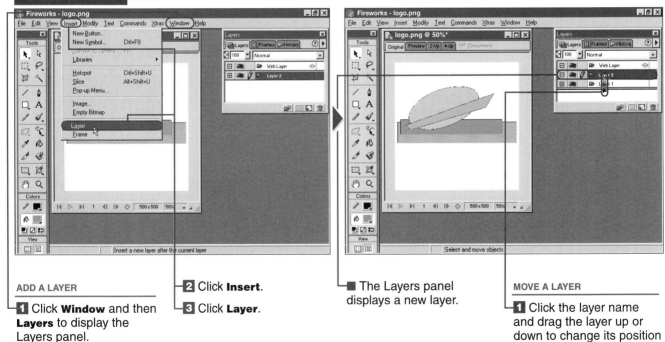

ADD A LAYER

1 Click **Window** and then **Layers** to display the Layers panel.

2 Click **Insert**.

3 Click **Layer**.

■ The Layers panel displays a new layer.

MOVE A LAYER

1 Click the layer name and drag the layer up or down to change its position in the stack.

82

What is the Web layer?

The Web layer is a special layer used just for slices and hotspots. See Chapters 8 and 9 for more information.

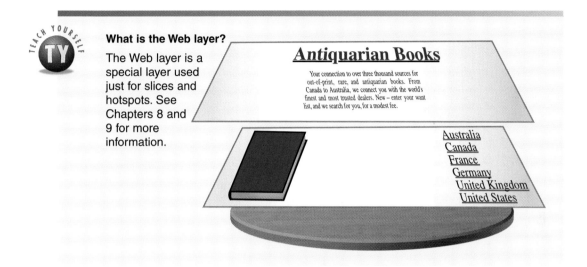

Antiquarian Books

Your connection to over three thousand sources for out-of-print, rare, and antiquarian books. From Canada to Australia, we connect you with the world's finest and most trusted dealers. New — enter your want list, and we search for you, for a modest fee.

Australia
Canada
France
Germany
United Kingdom
United States

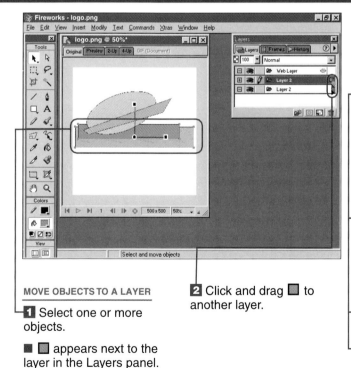

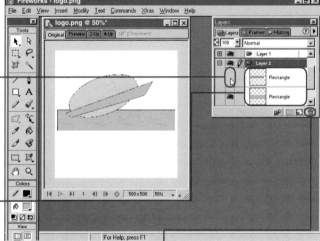

MOVE OBJECTS TO A LAYER

1 Select one or more objects.

■ ▨ appears next to the layer in the Layers panel.

2 Click and drag ▨ to another layer.

HIDE OR DELETE A LAYER

■ Multiple objects in a layer create sublayers.

1 Click ▨ for the layer or sublayer that you want to hide.

■ The ▨ disappears from its box, and the layer is hidden.

■ You can delete a layer by selecting it in the Layers panel and clicking the Delete Layer button (🗑).

IMPORT AN OBJECT

You can import objects you created in other applications, such as Adobe Illustrator.

When importing BMP, JPEG, GIF, and TIFF images, you can follow these same steps.

IMPORT AN OBJECT

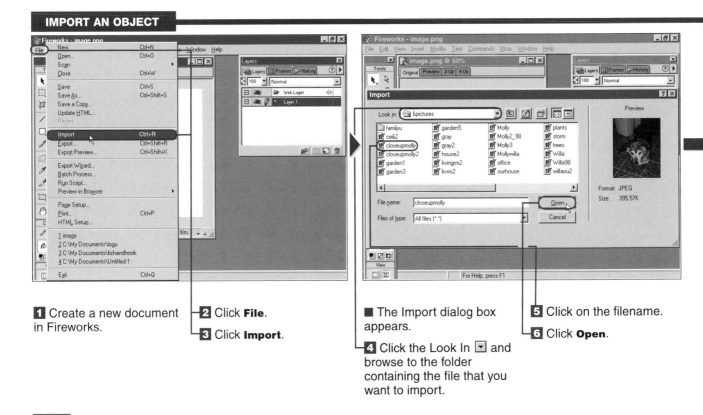

1 Create a new document in Fireworks.

2 Click **File**.

3 Click **Import**.

■ The Import dialog box appears.

4 Click the Look In ▼ and browse to the folder containing the file that you want to import.

5 Click on the filename.

6 Click **Open**.

How do I import an object with layers?

You can import objects from applications that apply layers, such as Photoshop. Fireworks displays an additional dialog box after you import. The dialog box contains options for using layers, such as Maintain Layers and Share Layers.

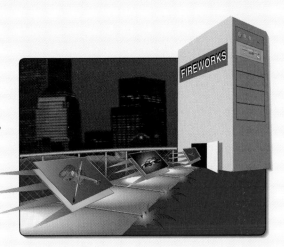

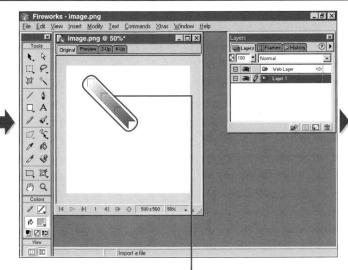

■ ⌖ changes to the import cursor (⌐).

■ You can click and drag the cursor to specify the final size of the object.

7 Click the page to insert the object at its original size.

CHAPTER 5

Working with Images

Are you ready to edit and modify your pictures? This chapter shows you how to work with images.

UNDERSTAND IMAGE MODE

You can edit images in Fireworks in image edit mode. The tools you use and the type of pictures define image mode. Fireworks automatically changes to image mode when you choose an image-editing tool.

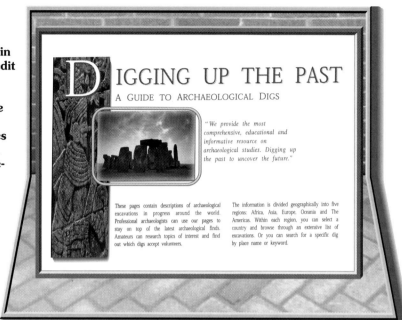

For information about importing an image, see Chapter 4.

VECTOR DRAWING

Fireworks is basically a *vector drawing* program. Vector drawing defines paths, as opposed to images, and uses object mode.

BITMAP IMAGES

A *bitmap* describes an image from a scanner or digital camera. Fireworks uses image mode, with special tools, to edit bitmap images.

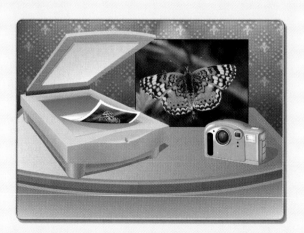

UNDERSTAND PIXELS

Bitmaps are made up of *pixels*. A pixel is the smallest unit of a bitmap.

EDIT PIXELS

You can edit individual or groups of pixels in a bitmap. For example, you can change the color of pixels, or you can blur them.

PIXELS AND VECTORS

Fireworks provides pixel bitmaps for use with vector objects. You can draw a circle and then use a bitmap to fill the object. You can edit pixels in any bitmap.

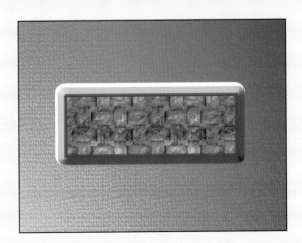

MODIFY THE IMAGE

You can modify an image's size to make it fit the space on your Web page.

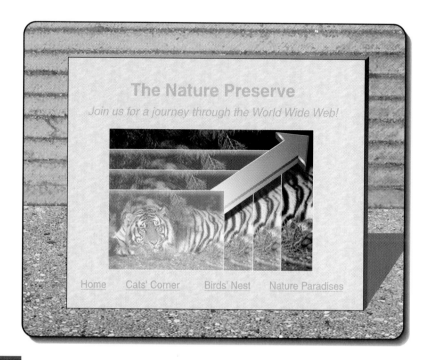

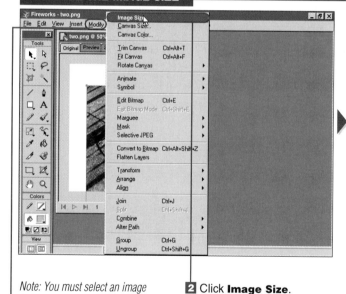

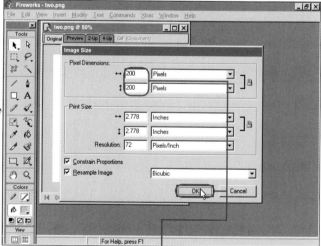

Note: You must select an image before you can modify it.

1 Click **Modify**.

2 Click **Image Size**.

■ The Image Size dialog box appears.

Note: If the image is for use on a Web page, use the pixel dimensions to set the size.

3 Type the new size in pixels.

4 Click **OK**.

What is the difference between the pixel dimensions and the print size?

The pixel dimension defines the number of pixels in the image, which describes the size of the image on-screen. The print size defines the size of the image if you printed it.

SET THE PRINT SIZE

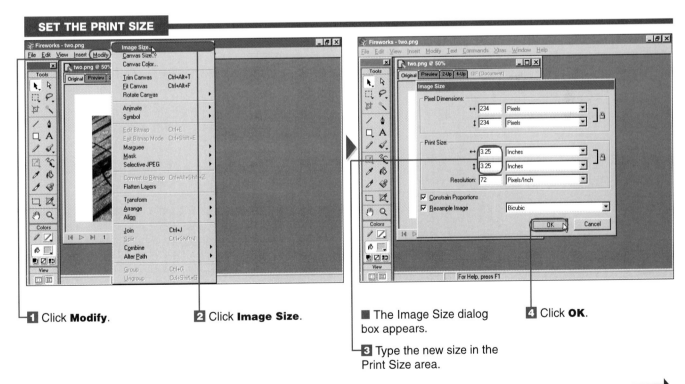

1 Click **Modify**.

2 Click **Image Size**.

■ The Image Size dialog box appears.

3 Type the new size in the Print Size area.

4 Click **OK**.

CONTINUED

MODIFY THE IMAGE

You can set the on-screen or printed resolution of the image to change its size or quality.

SET THE IMAGE RESOLUTION

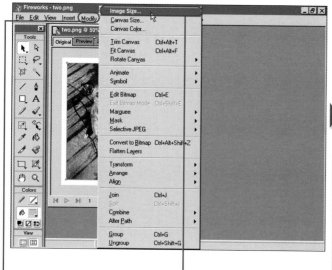

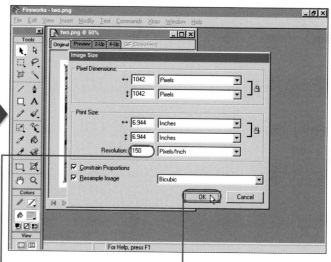

1 Click **Modify**.

2 Click **Image Size**.

■ The Image Size dialog box appears.

3 Type in the new resolution.

Note: When you change the resolution, the pixel dimensions change as well.

4 Click **OK**.

What does resolution control?

Resolution for an online image sets the size of the image. The higher the resolution, the larger the image. Resolution for a printed image, however, determines the quality of the image.

CONSTRAIN THE PROPORTIONS

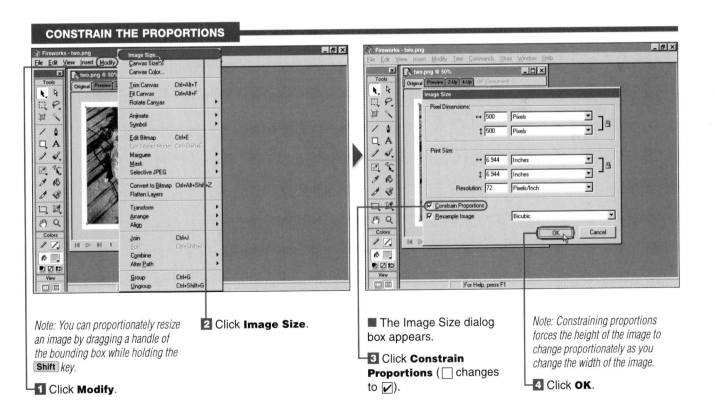

Note: You can proportionately resize an image by dragging a handle of the bounding box while holding the **Shift** *key.*

1 Click **Modify**.

2 Click **Image Size**.

■ The Image Size dialog box appears.

3 Click **Constrain Proportions** (☐ changes to ☑).

Note: Constraining proportions forces the height of the image to change proportionately as you change the width of the image.

4 Click **OK**.

CROP AN IMAGE

You can crop an image to remove unwanted parts of the image.

CROP AN IMAGE

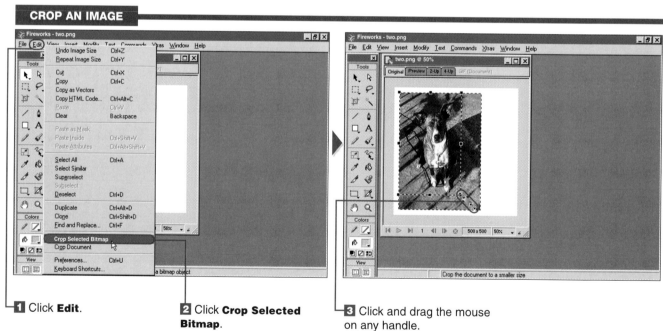

1 Click **Edit**.

2 Click **Crop Selected Bitmap**.

3 Click and drag the mouse on any handle.

When would I crop an image?

Crop an image when you want to remove an item or part of the image from a picture. For example, you may want to crop a picture if you took it from too far away.

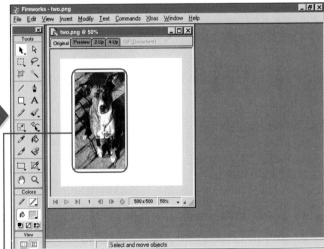

4 Click and drag other handles to finish setting the area that you want to crop to.

5 Double-click the image.

■ The image is cropped.

SELECT AND MOVE PIXELS

Although you can select an image with the mouse pointer, you can also select an entire image or a part of it with the Marquee or Lasso tools.

SELECT AND MOVE PIXELS WITH A MARQUEE

1 Click and hold the Marquee tool button (▦).

■ The ▦ and ⊙ buttons appear.

2 Click the shape you want to use.

■ ▷ changes to +.

3 Click and drag to select the shape.

4 Click the Pointer tool (▶).

5 Click the selected pixels and drag them to a new location.

**What is the difference between
the Marquee and Lasso tools?**

The Marquee tool creates a
rectangular, square, oval, or
circular shape. The Lasso tool
creates natural irregular shapes,
and the polygonal lasso creates
angular irregular shapes.

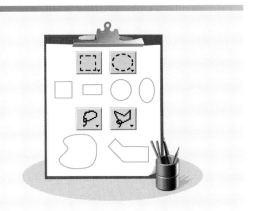

SELECT AND MOVE PIXELS WITH A LASSO

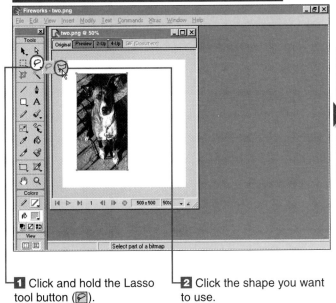

1 Click and hold the Lasso
tool button (⬭).

2 Click the shape you want
to use.

3 Draw the area with the
Lasso tool.

4 Click ⬉.

5 Click and drag the area to
another area of the
document.

*Note: You can double-click the tool
to exit lasso mode.*

CONTINUED

SELECT AND MOVE PIXELS

You can select certain colors of pixels to remove them from the picture. For example, you can use the magic wand to remove a background.

SELECT PIXELS WITH THE MAGIC WAND

1 Click the Magic Wand tool (◥).

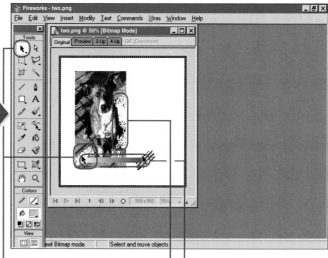

■ ⬚ changes to ✎.

2 Click the magic wand on the color of pixel you want to select.

3 Click ◥.

4 Click and drag the pixels to another area.

■ You can press Delete to remove the selected pixels.

98

**What do I do with the pixels
I cut?**

You can move the cut pixels
to another part of the
document or to another
document by using the cut
and paste commands. You
can also cut the selected
pixels to remove them from
the image completely.

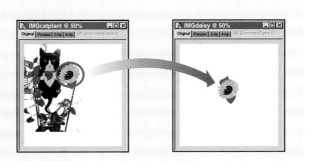

SELECT MULTIPLE AREAS

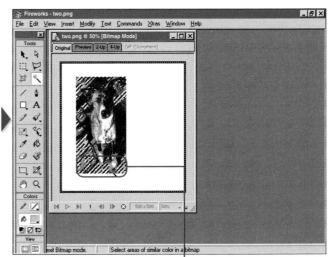

■1 Click 🔲, 🔲, or 🔲.

■2 Click the first area in
the image.

■3 Press and hold the Shift
key.

*Note: You can press and hold the
Alt (option) key instead if you
want to deselect areas.*

■4 Select the other areas to
be copied, moved, or
removed.

ERASE PIXELS

You can erase pixels
from an image with the
Eraser tool.

The Eraser tool works just
like a pencil eraser, but on
images only.

–1 Click the Eraser tool
button (✐).

■ ↳ changes to ✐.

■ You can double-click ✐ to
display the Tool Options
(Eraser Tool) panel.

–2 Click the Eraser Size ▼
and drag the slider to
change the size of the
eraser point.

–3 Click ■ or ● to change
the shape of the eraser.

–4 Click and drag the Edge
Softness slider to change
the edge.

**Why does the area I erased look
like a checkerboard?**

The checkerboard indicates that
the area is transparent. You can
change the erased area to the
canvas color or fill the area with a
color of your choice.

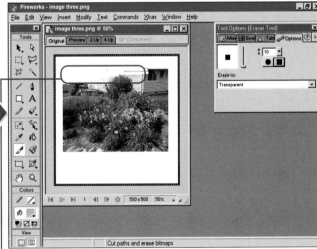

5 Click the Eraser Color ▼.

6 Choose the option to
erase to.

*Note: If you choose **Transparent**,
for example, the pixels you erase
become transparent.*

7 Click and drag back and
forth to erase pixels.

ADJUST BRIGHTNESS AND CONTRAST

You can adjust the brightness and contrast of an image when the image is too dark or lacks clarity.

ADJUST BRIGHTNESS AND CONTRAST

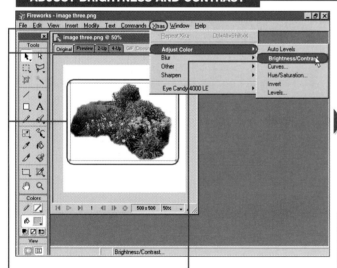

1 Select the image.

2 Click **Xtras**.

3 Click **Adjust Color**.

4 Click **Brightness/Contrast**.

■ The Brightness/Contrast dialog box appears.

■ You can move the Brightness/Contrast dialog box down and to the right of the image and click **Preview** (☐ changes to ✔) if you want to preview your brightness and contrast changes as you make them.

5 Click and drag the Brightness slider.

How much can I adjust brightness or contrast?

Values for the brightness and contrast sliders range from-100 to 100. If an image requires more adjustment than-100 or 100, consider using another photograph.

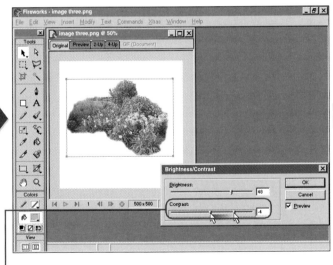

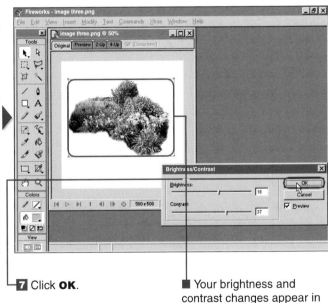

6 Click and drag the Contrast slider.

Note: You can experiment with the contrast and brightness while you view the changes in the document.

7 Click **OK**.

■ Your brightness and contrast changes appear in the image.

BLUR AN IMAGE

You can blur an image to give it an unfocused effect.

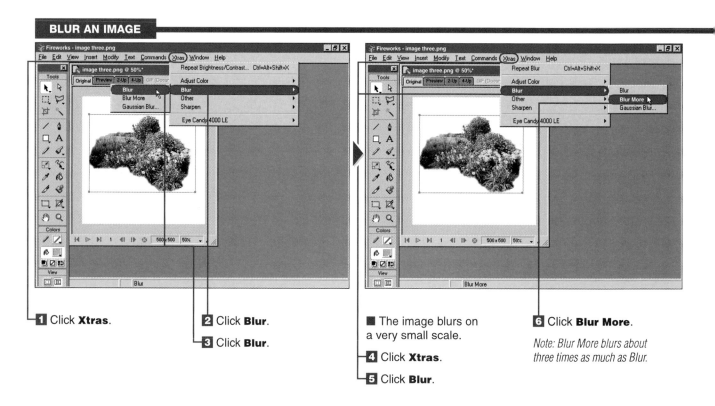

1 Click **Xtras**.

2 Click **Blur**.

3 Click **Blur**.

■ The image blurs on a very small scale.

4 Click **Xtras**.

5 Click **Blur**.

6 Click **Blur More**.

Note: Blur More blurs about three times as much as Blur.

What is a Gaussian blur?

The Gaussian Blur command applies a specific amount of blur to each pixel of the image, giving the image a hazy effect. You can adjust the Gaussian blur to make the image into colors instead of shapes.

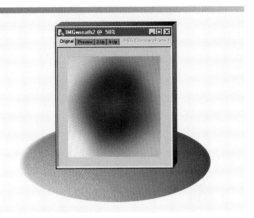

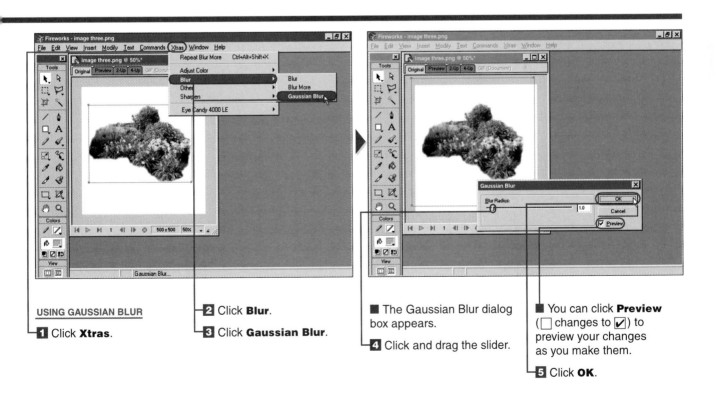

USING GAUSSIAN BLUR

1 Click **Xtras**.

2 Click **Blur**.

3 Click **Gaussian Blur**.

■ The Gaussian Blur dialog box appears.

4 Click and drag the slider.

■ You can click **Preview** (☐ changes to ☑) to preview your changes as you make them.

5 Click **OK**.

SHARPEN AN IMAGE

You can sharpen an image to bring out details and edges in your image.

SHARPEN AN IMAGE

1 Click **Xtras**.

2 Click **Sharpen**.

3 Click **Sharpen**.

■ The image sharpens on a small scale.

4 Click **Xtras**.

5 Click **Sharpen**.

6 Click **Sharpen More**.

Note: Sharpen More sharpens about three times as much as Sharpen.

What is Unsharp Mask?

The Unsharp Mask command sharpens the edges of the image by adding more contrast. Unsharp Mask offers the most control in the pixel radius — which sharpens each pixel's edge.

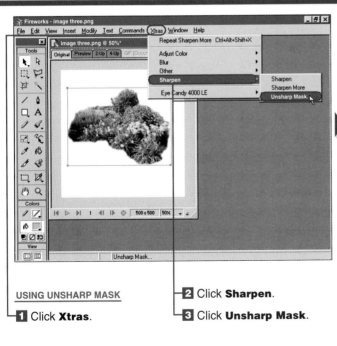

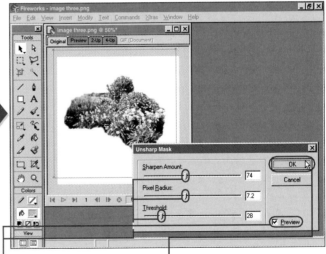

USING UNSHARP MASK

1 Click **Xtras**.

2 Click **Sharpen**.

3 Click **Unsharp Mask**.

■ The Unsharp Mask dialog box appears.

■ You can click **Preview** to preview changes in the image.

4 Click and drag one of the sliders.

Note: **Sharpen Amount** determines the percentage of sharpness, **Pixel Radius** sharpens contrast around pixels' edges, and **Threshold** sharpens only high contrast pixels.

5 Click **OK**.

CONVERT AN IMAGE

You can change any
image from full color to
grayscale or sepia tones
if you want your image
to look aged.

CONVERT AN IMAGE

TO GRAYSCALE

-1 Click **Commands**.

-2 Click **Creative**.

-3 Click **Convert to
Grayscale**.

-4 Click **Window** and then
Swatches to display the
Swatches panel.

-5 Click the Option ▶.

-6 Click **Grayscale**.

■ You can edit the pixels
using grayscale swatches.

When would I use grayscale or sepia tone in a Web page?

You can use grayscale or sepia when you want to create an animated GIF to export to your Web page. See Chapter 11 for more information about animations.

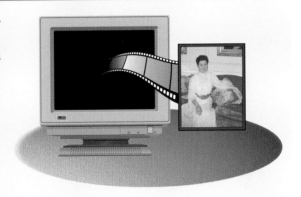

TO SEPIA TONE

1 Click **Commands**.

2 Click **Creative**.

3 Click **Convert to Sepia Tone**.

■ The image changes to sepia tones.

Note: There is no preset sepia color swatch set.

OUTER GLOW

Edit Mask

Selecting
Masked
Object

Live Effects

...APPLYING DROP SHADOW...

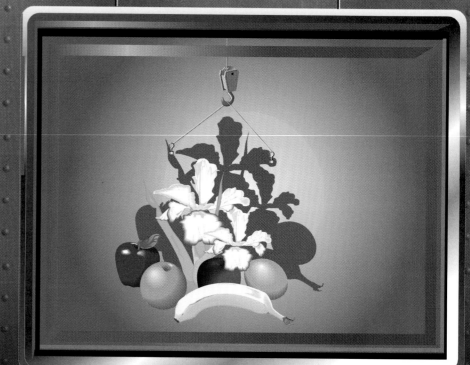

COLOR

SHARPEN

B

BEV

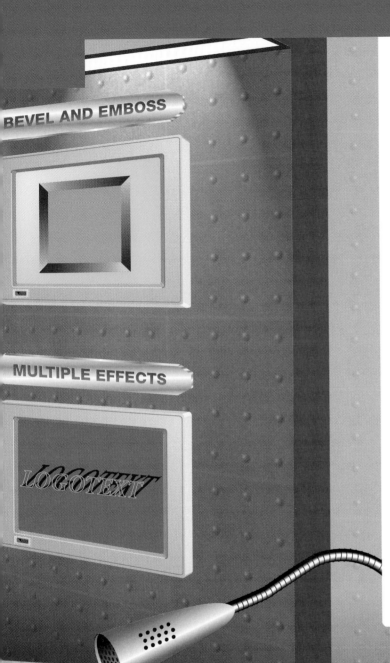

BEVEL AND EMBOSS

MULTIPLE EFFECTS

LOGOTEXT

CHAPTER 6

Apply Effects

Do you want to make your text and objects look more exciting and interesting? This chapter shows you how to apply effects to your graphics.

EMBOSS   SHADOW

DEPTH   SET DEFAULTS

INNER
GLOW   OUTER
GLOW   SAVE
STYLE

UNDERSTAND LIVE EFFECTS

You create effects in text and objects by drawing shadows, beveled edges, or other designs that enhance the object. Effects are called "live" because Fireworks redraws the object on the screen each time you edit it.

After you apply effects to text and objects, you can also edit or remove the effects as easily as you applied them.

Effects can add the illusion of motion to objects and text. Blurs make the object look like it is moving. Glows make the object look alive. Color changes make the object vibrant.

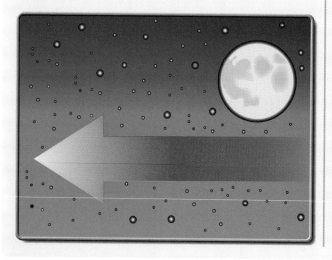

THREE-DIMENSIONAL APPEARANCE

Effects can make the items on the page look three-dimensional. All objects have height and width. The third dimension is depth. Shadows and other effects add depth to text and to objects.

BEVEL

A bevel is an angled edge added to the surface of text or an object to give the object depth.

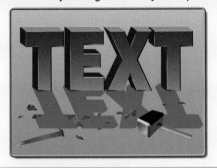

EMBOSS

Embossing is a way to add an indistinct shadow to an object or text.

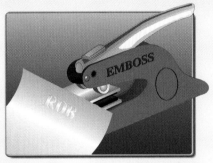

BLUR AND SHARPEN

A blur makes the outline of the text or object unclear. Sharpening the object makes the edges more distinct.

SHADOW

Shadows add depth to any object or text by making it look like a light is shining on one side of the object.

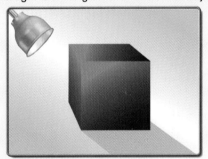

GLOW

A glow adds a light around the outside of the object, leaving the edges perfectly sharp and clear.

COLOR

Color effects include brightness, contrast, hue, and other color characteristics. You can use color effects on objects, text, and images. For more information about color, see Chapter 12.

BEVEL AND EMBOSS EDGES

You can apply two popular effects — bevel and emboss — to buttons and other graphics so that the graphics look three-dimensional.

BEVEL EDGES

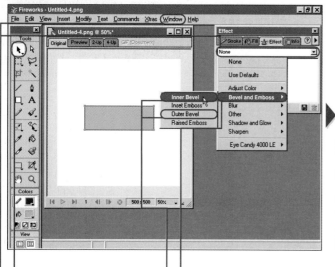

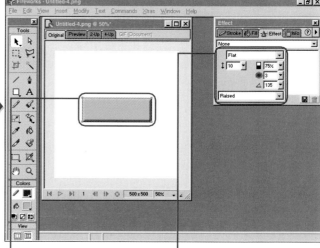

1 Use 🔲 to select the object.

2 Click **Window** and then **Effect** to display the Effect panel.

3 Click the Effect 🔽.

4 Click **Bevel and Emboss**.

5 Click **Inner Bevel** or **Outer Bevel**.

Note: Inner Bevel adds a 3D border around the inside of the object, and Outer Bevel adds a 3D border around the outside of the object.

■ The button is beveled.

■ You can adjust the bevel slope, width, and other options in the box that appears.

What is the difference between bevel and emboss?

The bevel applies an angled edge to either the inside or the outside of the object. Embossing adds highlights or shadows to the object to make it appear pushed in or out of the background.

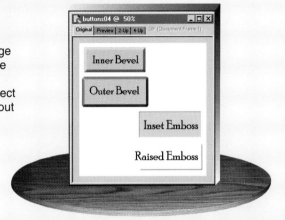

EMBOSS EDGES

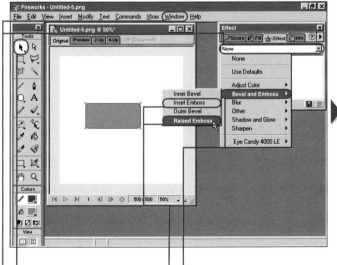

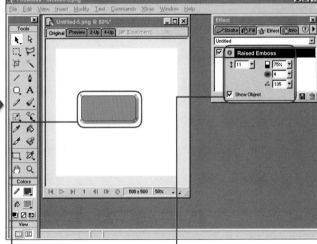

1 Use to select the object.

2 Click **Window** and then **Effect** to display the Effect panel.

3 Click the Effect ⏷.

4 Click **Bevel and Emboss**.

5 Click **Inset Emboss** or **Raised Emboss**.

Note: Inset Emboss looks like the object is embedded in the page. Raised Emboss looks like the button is hovering over the page.

■ The object is embossed.

■ You can adjust the emboss slope, width, and other options in the box that appears.

BLUR AND SHARPEN EDGES

You can blur or
sharpen the edges to
make certain objects
stand out in a
graphic.

To find out how to
blur or sharpen an
entire image instead
of just the edges,
refer to Chapter 5.

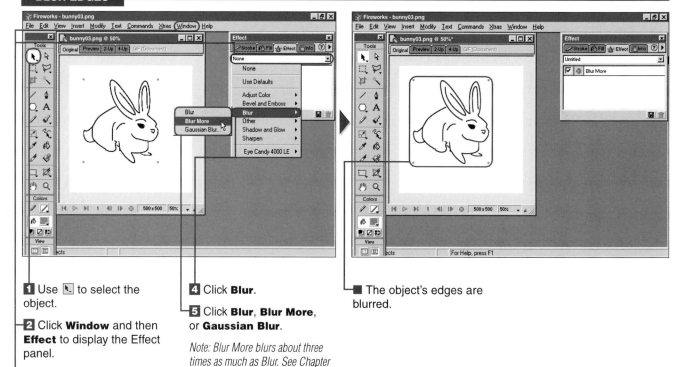

1 Use to select the
object.

2 Click **Window** and then
Effect to display the Effect
panel.

3 Click the Effect ▾.

4 Click **Blur**.

5 Click **Blur**, **Blur More**,
or **Gaussian Blur**.

*Note: Blur More blurs about three
times as much as Blur. See Chapter
5 for more information about
Gaussian Blur.*

■ The object's edges are
blurred.

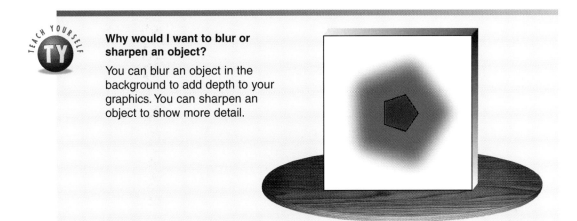

Why would I want to blur or sharpen an object?

You can blur an object in the background to add depth to your graphics. You can sharpen an object to show more detail.

SHARPEN EDGES

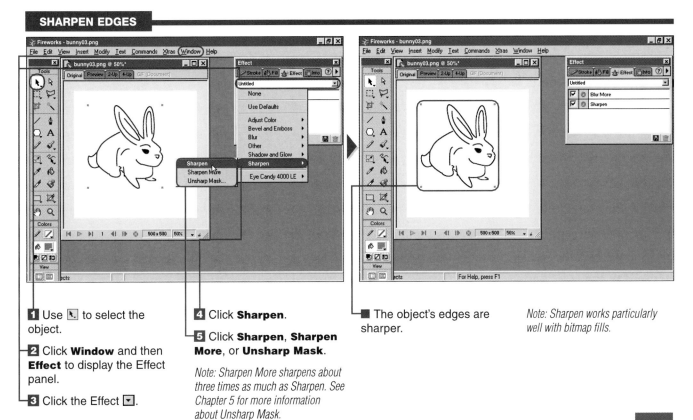

1 Use ☒ to select the object.

2 Click **Window** and then **Effect** to display the Effect panel.

3 Click the Effect ▾.

4 Click **Sharpen**.

5 Click **Sharpen**, **Sharpen More**, or **Unsharp Mask**.

Note: Sharpen More sharpens about three times as much as Sharpen. See Chapter 5 for more information about Unsharp Mask.

■ The object's edges are sharper.

Note: Sharpen works particularly well with bitmap fills.

APPLY A SHADOW

You can add a shadow to a button or other object. Shadows add depth to the graphic.

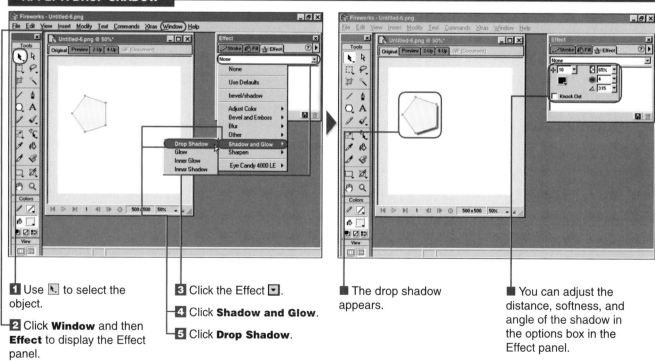

1 Use to select the object.

2 Click **Window** and then **Effect** to display the Effect panel.

3 Click the Effect ▼.

4 Click **Shadow and Glow**.

5 Click **Drop Shadow**.

■ The drop shadow appears.

■ You can adjust the distance, softness, and angle of the shadow in the options box in the Effect panel.

What is the difference between a drop shadow and an inner shadow?

A drop shadow is a copy of the object offset to the outside of the object to give the illusion of depth. An inner shadow is similar but the shadow is on the inside of the object. Shadows only appear on one or two sides.

APPLY AN INNER SHADOW

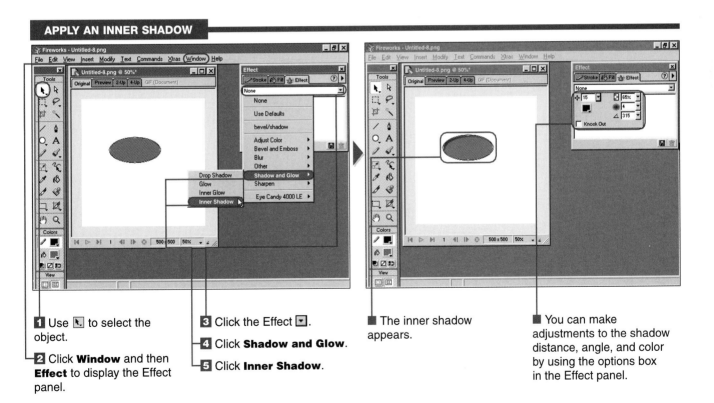

1 Use [icon] to select the object.

2 Click **Window** and then **Effect** to display the Effect panel.

3 Click the Effect [icon].

4 Click **Shadow and Glow**.

5 Click **Inner Shadow**.

■ The inner shadow appears.

■ You can make adjustments to the shadow distance, angle, and color by using the options box in the Effect panel.

APPLY A GLOW

You can apply a glow
that gives the object a
border around all edges.

APPLY A GLOW

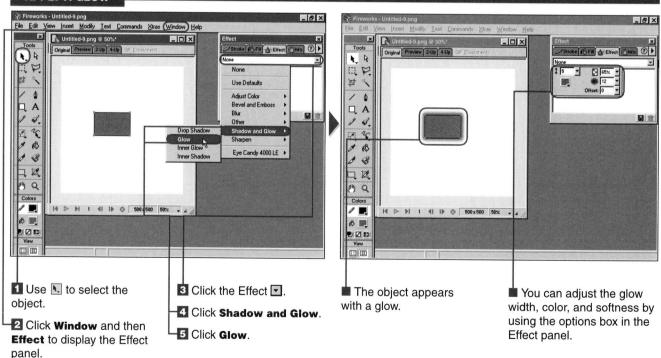

1 Use ![cursor] to select the object.

2 Click **Window** and then **Effect** to display the Effect panel.

3 Click the Effect ![dropdown].

4 Click **Shadow and Glow**.

5 Click **Glow**.

■ The object appears with a glow.

■ You can adjust the glow width, color, and softness by using the options box in the Effect panel.

What is the difference between a glow and an inner glow?

A glow is a border on the outside of the object making the object look raised from the page. An inner glow appears on the inside of the object's edges, making the object look recessed on the page.

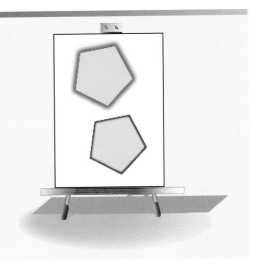

APPLY AN INNER GLOW

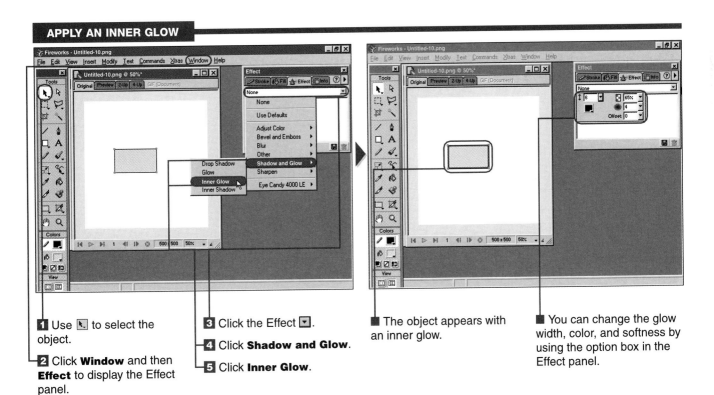

1 Use ▣ to select the object.

2 Click **Window** and then **Effect** to display the Effect panel.

3 Click the Effect ▣.

4 Click **Shadow and Glow**.

5 Click **Inner Glow**.

■ The object appears with an inner glow.

■ You can change the glow width, color, and softness by using the option box in the Effect panel.

APPLY MULTIPLE EFFECTS

You can add multiple effects to an object to give the object depth, variety, and more interest.

Fireworks makes it easy to add effects to and remove effects from an object.

APPLY MULTIPLE EFFECTS

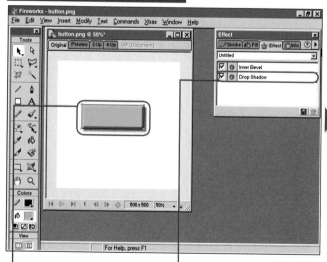

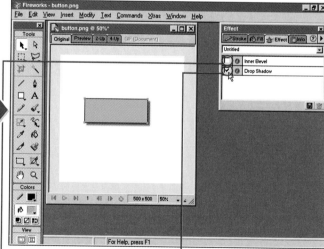

1 Apply an effect to the selected object (such as Inner Bevel).

Note: See the section "Bevel and Emboss Edges" for more information about applying Inner Bevel.

2 Apply another effect to the object (such as Drop Shadow).

Note: See the section "Apply a Shadow" for more information about applying Drop Shadow.

3 Click unchecked effects that you want to keep (☐ changes to ☑).

4 Click checked effects that you want to remove (☑ changes to ☐).

How can I best use multiple effects on an object?

Use only one or two effects on each object. Repeat the exact same effects on other objects in the group to give all objects a similar appearance.

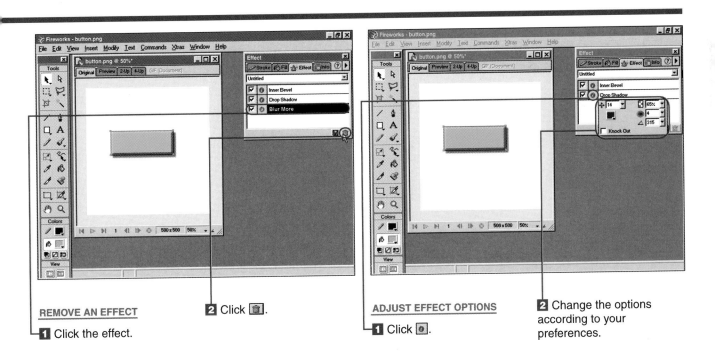

REMOVE AN EFFECT

1 Click the effect.

2 Click 🗑.

ADJUST EFFECT OPTIONS

1 Click 🔘.

2 Change the options according to your preferences.

SET DEFAULTS

You can set default effects that you can apply to new objects, which enables you to format objects quickly and easily.

A *default* is a characteristic that you can assign to a graphic.

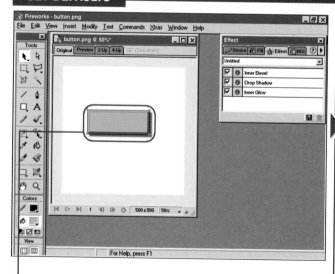

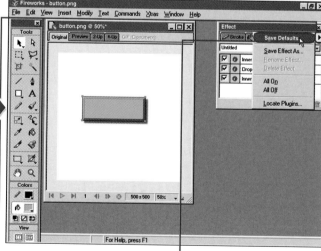

1 Apply the effects that you want to use as defaults to the object.

Note: You can change options for each effect, such as color and angle.

2 Click the Options ▶.

3 Click **Save Defaults**.

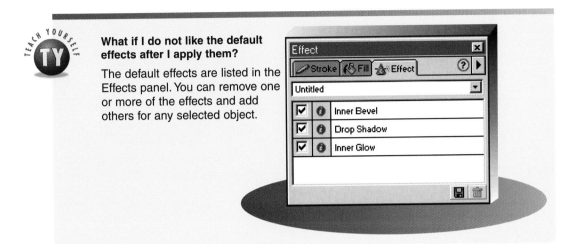

What if I do not like the default effects after I apply them?

The default effects are listed in the Effects panel. You can remove one or more of the effects and add others for any selected object.

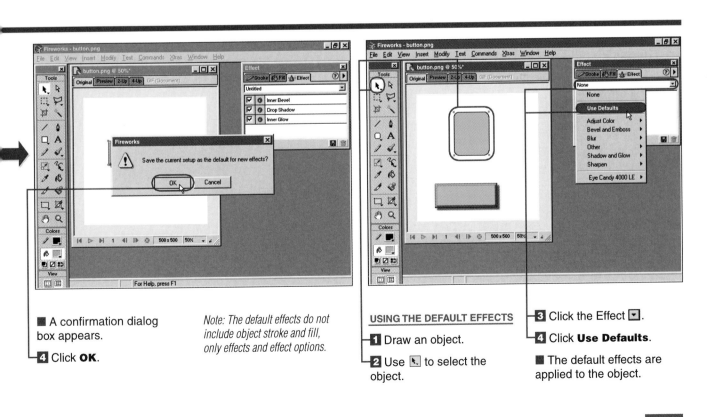

■ A confirmation dialog box appears.

◢4 Click **OK**.

Note: The default effects do not include object stroke and fill, only effects and effect options.

USING THE DEFAULT EFFECTS

◢1 Draw an object.

◢2 Use ▣ to select the object.

◢3 Click the Effect ▣.

◢4 Click **Use Defaults**.

■ The default effects are applied to the object.

SAVE A CUSTOM EFFECT

You can save a
custom effect for
use with graphics
in other Fireworks
documents.

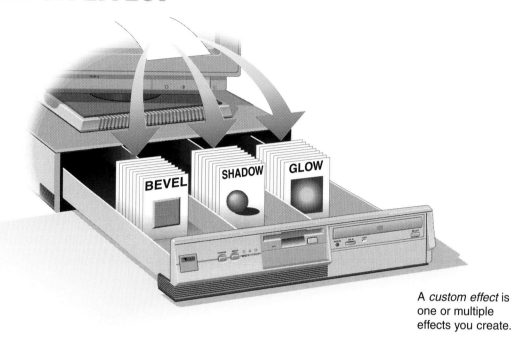

A *custom effect* is
one or multiple
effects you create.

SAVE A CUSTOM EFFECT

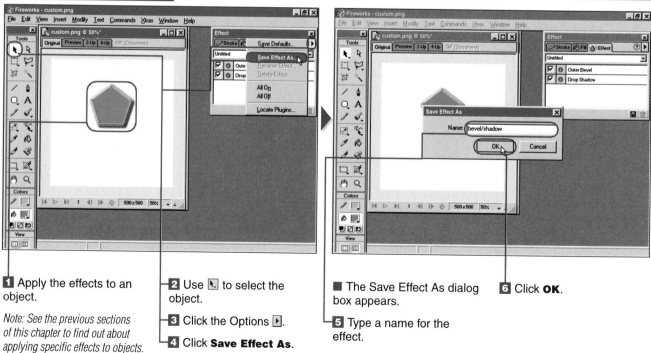

1 Apply the effects to an
object.

*Note: See the previous sections
of this chapter to find out about
applying specific effects to objects.*

2 Use ⬚ to select the
object.

3 Click the Options ▶.

4 Click **Save Effect As**.

■ The Save Effect As dialog
box appears.

5 Type a name for the
effect.

6 Click **OK**.

Can I remove a custom effect from the Options pop-up menu?

Yes. Apply the effect to an object. Then, click the Options ⬛ and click **Delete Effect**.

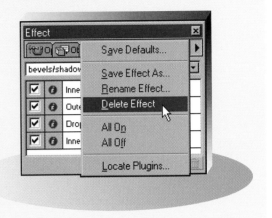

USING A CUSTOM EFFECT

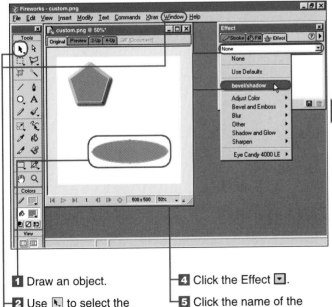

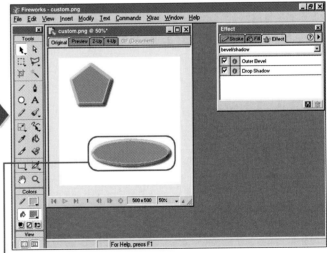

■1 Draw an object.

■2 Use ▦ to select the object.

■3 Click **Window** and then **Effect** to display the Effect panel.

■4 Click the Effect ▾.

■5 Click the name of the custom effect.

■ The custom effect appears on the object.

Note: The custom effects appear in the Effect panel. You can add or remove custom effects.

SAVE AND USE STYLES

You can use styles to save custom effects, fills, strokes, and text characteristics.

After you save a style, you can apply that style to another object with one click of the mouse.

SAVE STYLES

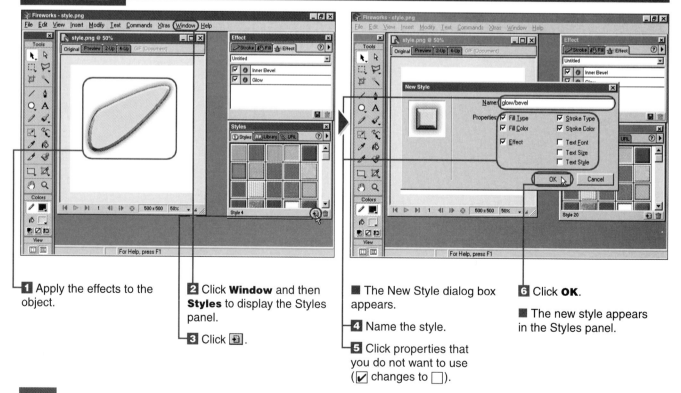

1 Apply the effects to the object.

2 Click **Window** and then **Styles** to display the Styles panel.

3 Click 🔁.

■ The New Style dialog box appears.

4 Name the style.

5 Click properties that you do not want to use (☑ changes to ☐).

6 Click **OK**.

■ The new style appears in the Styles panel.

What are the other styles in the Styles panel?

Fireworks provides a variety of preset styles that you can use on your text and objects. You can apply any style in the Styles panel by following the steps in "Using Styles."

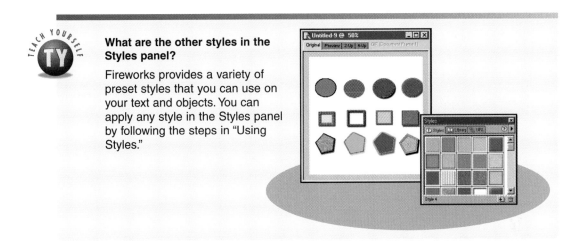

USING STYLES

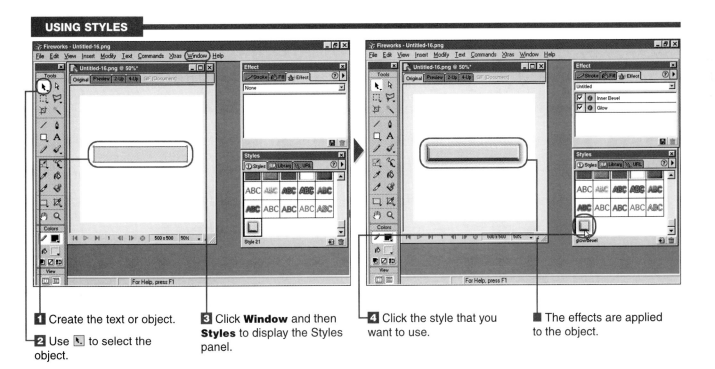

1 Create the text or object.

2 Use ▶ to select the object.

3 Click **Window** and then **Styles** to display the Styles panel.

4 Click the style that you want to use.

■ The effects are applied to the object.

CREATE MASKS

You can create a cut-out effect on an underlying image by creating a mask.

The mask blocks out part of the underlying image.

CREATE MASKS

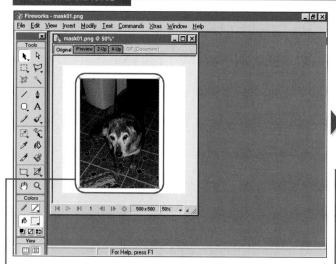

1 Create the object or import the image to be masked.

Note: For information about importing objects, refer to Chapter 4.

2 Create the object to be used as a mask.

3 Choose a pattern or texture for the mask or choose no fill.

Note: See Chapter 4 for information about applying a pattern or texture.

What are some common uses for masks?

You can create text with a gradient fill, blend an image into a background of patterns, or add a blurred frame to an image. Experiment with masking to create unusual effects.

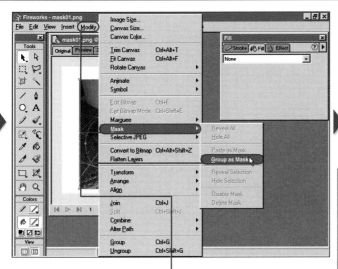

▣ Select both objects.

Note: Press and hold the Shift *key to select multiple objects.*

▬ 5 Click **Modify**.

▬ 6 Click **Mask**.

▬ 7 Click **Group as Mask**.

■ The masked image appears.

■ You can click and drag the mask group handle to reposition the object within the mask.

EDIT MASKS

You can modify the masked group at any time in Fireworks. You first must select an object to edit it.

A *masked group* refers to the topmost object that is used as a mask plus the object that is masked.

SELECT OBJECTS WITHIN A MASK

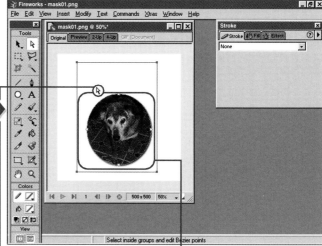

1 Click the Subselection tool (▶).

Note: The Subselection tool lets you locate grouped and masked objects.

2 Position the cursor over the masked group.

Note: Selected objects are outlined in blue. Other objects are outlined in red.

3 Click the object that you want to edit.

When I select a masked group, which object's formatting shows up in the Effect panel?

When you select a masked group, the top object's attributes show up in the Fill panel, the Stroke panel, and the Effect panel.

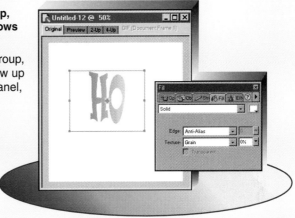

EDIT THE MASK

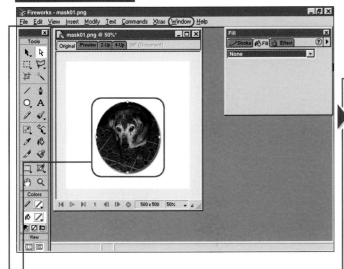

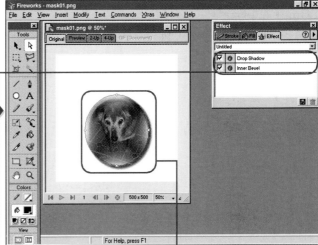

1 Select the masked object or the mask.

2 Click **Window** and then **Fill**, **Stroke**, or **Effect** to display the Fill, Stroke, or Effect panel.

Note: You can add stroke, fill, or an effect to the mask to make it more interesting.

3 Make the changes that you want to the selected object.

■ Changes appear without unmasking the group.

CHAPTER 7

Create Buttons and Navigation Bars

Are you ready to make your graphics into working buttons? This chapter shows you how.

UNDERSTAND BUTTONS AND NAVIGATION BARS

You can use buttons and navigation bars to move around a Web page and a Web site.

BUTTONS

You use buttons on a Web page to perform an action, such as jumping to another Web page.

NAVIGATION BARS

A *navigation bar* is a group of buttons that helps you find your way around a Web site. The navigation bar remains on the page when other elements of the page change.

UP STATE

The *up state* of a button is the way the button looks before you click it. Up state is the default.

DOWN STATE

The *down state* of the button is the way it looks after it has been clicked.

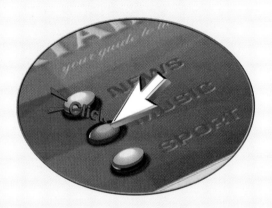

SYMBOLS AND INSTANCES

A *symbol* represents an object, such as a button. An *instance* is a copy of the symbol that you can modify.

ROLLOVER

Rollover is a term that describes the change that takes place in a button when a user moves his or her mouse pointer over the button.

CREATE A BUTTON

You can create buttons that the user clicks to perform an action on the Web page, such as jumping to another Web page.

Format the button using effect tools or use a button symbol from the library that comes with Fireworks.

CREATE A BUTTON

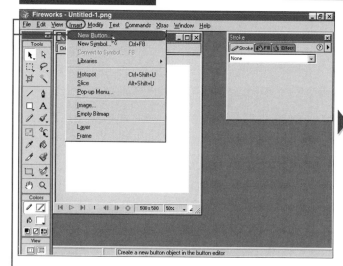

1 Click **Insert**.

2 Click **New Button**.

Note: You can also add a new symbol, which can be a button or a graphic.

■ The Button Editor dialog box appears.

3 Create a button on the Up tab.

■ Draw the button the way that you want it to look on your Web page; this is called the *up state*.

Note: See Chapters 4 and 6 for information about drawing graphics and applying effects.

■ You can use the Styles panel to format the button.

4 Click **Onion Skinning** (☐ changes to ☑).

5 Click the **Down** tab.

What is Onion Skinning?

The Onion Skinning check box lets you see the up state button so that you can build the down state on top of it.

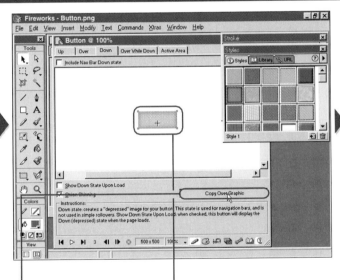

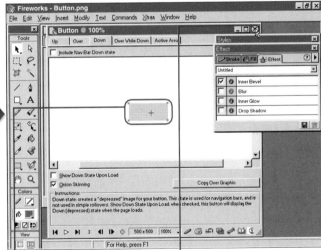

6 Click **Copy Over Graphic**.

■ An outline of the previous button appears. You can draw over the copy so that the button looks similar to the up state.

7 Create the button the way that you want it to look when it has been clicked.

Note: This is called the down state. *You can add an inner shadow or an emboss, for example (see Chapter 6).*

8 Click ⊠ to close the Button Editor.

■ The button symbol appears in the Library panel and an instance appears in your document.

CONVERT AN OBJECT TO A BUTTON

You can convert any object you create into a button and then copy the button to the Button Editor.

CONVERT AN OBJECT TO A BUTTON

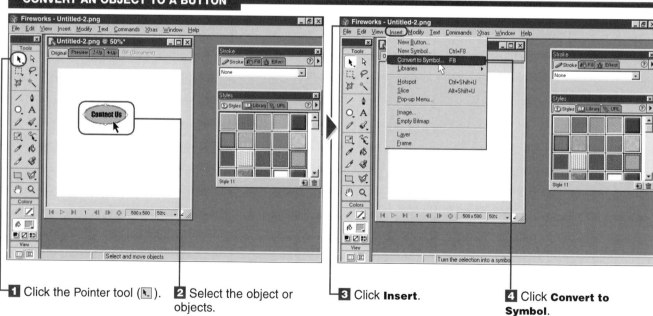

1 Click the Pointer tool (■).

2 Select the object or objects.

Note: See Chapter 4 for information about grouping multiple objects.

3 Click **Insert**.

4 Click **Convert to Symbol**.

What is a slice?

A *slice* is a part of a larger image. Slices are used to improve download time but also to create buttons for the Web. See Chapter 9 for more information.

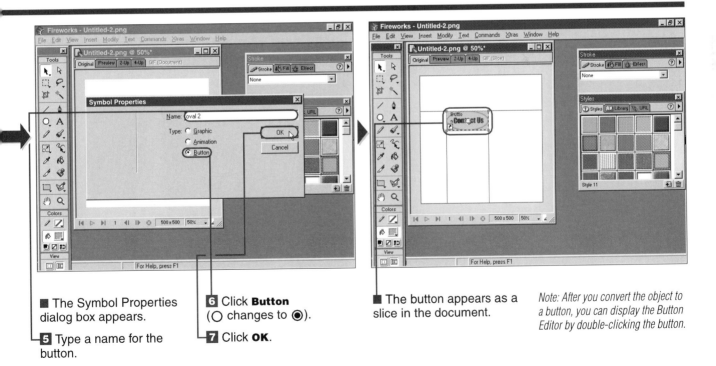

■ The Symbol Properties dialog box appears.

5 Type a name for the button.

6 Click **Button** (○ changes to ◉).

7 Click **OK**.

■ The button appears as a slice in the document.

Note: After you convert the object to a button, you can display the Button Editor by double-clicking the button.

COPY AND EDIT A BUTTON

You can copy a button and then edit it to change text or another part of the object.

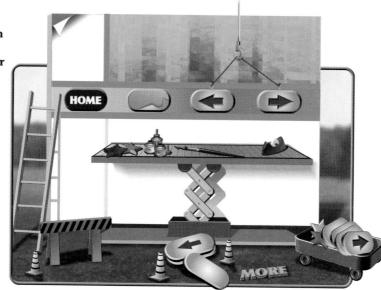

Copying a button means that all the buttons you create for one Web page will be similar in design and pattern.

COPY A BUTTON

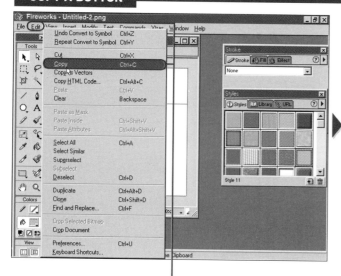

1 Select the button.

2 Click **Edit**.

3 Click **Copy**.

4 Open a new or existing document.

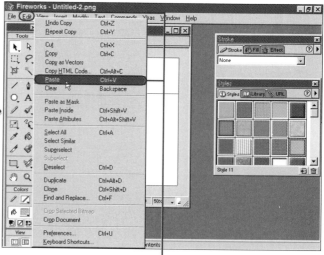

5 Click **Edit**.

6 Click **Paste**.

■ The copied button appears in the new document.

When I edit a copy of a button, does the original button change too?

No. You can edit an instance of a button. The original button does not change.

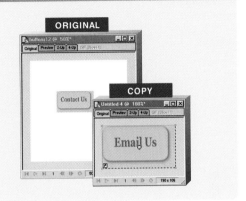

EDIT A BUTTON

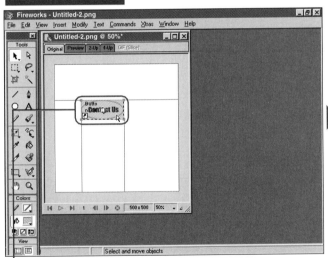

1 Double-click the button.

Note: If you copied the button, an information dialog box may appear. Click OK to continue.

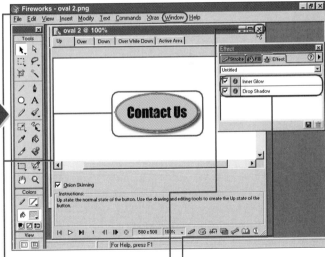

■ The Button Editor appears.

2 Select the object.

3 Click **Window** and then **Stroke**, **Fill**, or **Effect** to display the Stroke, Fill, or Effect panel or double-click the text, depending on the type of edits.

4 Make the changes that you want.

5 Click ⊠ to close the Button Editor.

ASSIGN A URL TO A BUTTON BY USING THE LINK WIZARD

You use the Link Wizard to assign a URL to buttons and other objects. The URL creates a link to another Web page.

URL stands for *Uniform Resource Locator* and is simply a Web address.

ASSIGN A URL TO A BUTTON BY USING THE LINK WIZARD

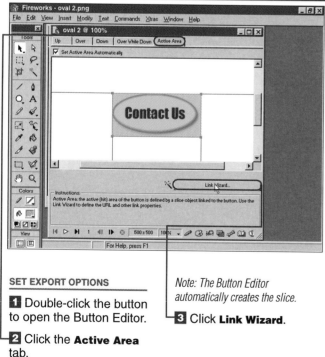

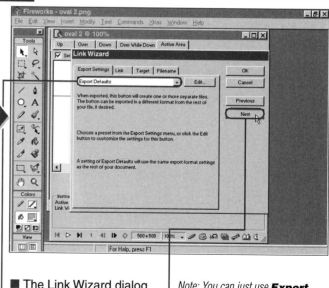

SET EXPORT OPTIONS

1 Double-click the button to open the Button Editor.

2 Click the **Active Area** tab.

Note: The Button Editor automatically creates the slice.

3 Click **Link Wizard**.

■ The Link Wizard dialog box appears.

4 Click ▾ and select an export setting.

*Note: You can just use **Export Defaults** if you prefer.*

5 Click **Next**.

What is the active area?

The *active area* is the part of the button that performs an action when clicked and is defined by creating a slice over the button. You can adjust the size of the slice if necessary.

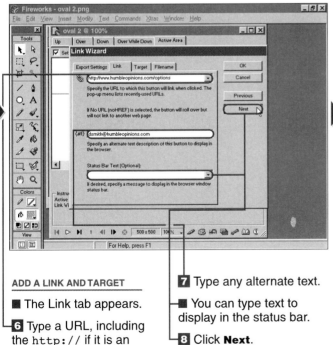

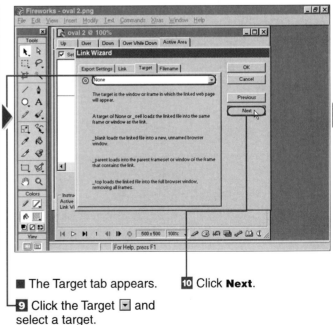

ADD A LINK AND TARGET

■ The Link tab appears.

6 Type a URL, including the http:// if it is an external URL.

7 Type any alternate text.

■ You can type text to display in the status bar.

8 Click **Next**.

■ The Target tab appears.

9 Click the Target ▼ and select a target.

*Note: Select **None** to load the link into the same window as the button.*

10 Click **Next**.

CONTINUED

ASSIGN A URL TO A BUTTON BY USING THE LINK WIZARD

You can use the Link
Wizard to create a
file consisting of the
sliced button and its
assigned URL.

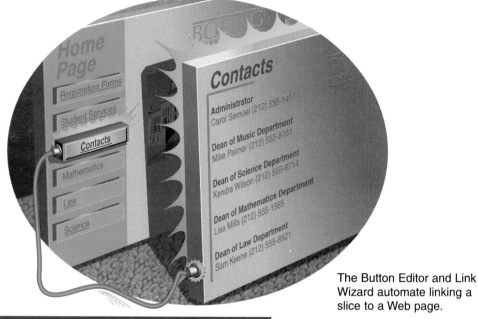

The Button Editor and Link
Wizard automate linking a
slice to a Web page.

ASSIGN A URL TO A BUTTON BY USING THE LINK WIZARD (CONTINUED)

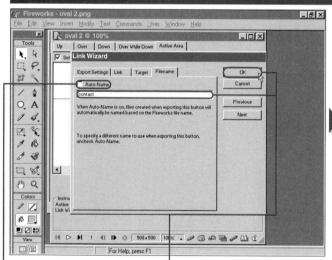

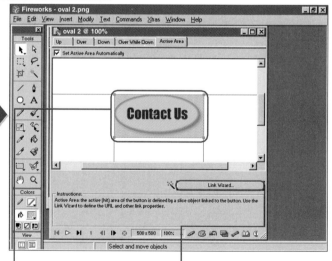

NAME A FILE

■ The Filename tab
appears.

11 Click **Auto-Name**
(☑ changes to ☐).

■ You can let Fireworks
automatically name files by
leaving Auto-Name
checked (☑), if you prefer.

12 Type a name for the
sliced file.

13 Click **OK**.

■ Fireworks displays the
button slice in the Button
Editor.

■ You can click **Link
Wizard** again to change
any settings in the Link
Wizard dialog box.

What is the URL Library?

The URL Library stores the URLs you add to it in the URL panel. You can use URLs listed in it for multiple buttons, slices, or hotspots.

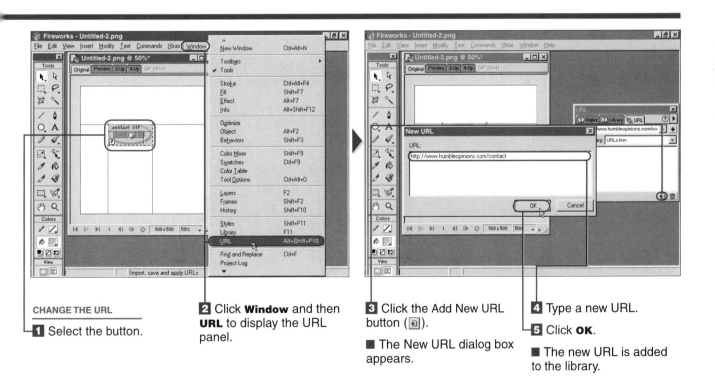

CHANGE THE URL

1 Select the button.

2 Click **Window** and then **URL** to display the URL panel.

3 Click the Add New URL button (⊞).

■ The New URL dialog box appears.

4 Type a new URL.

5 Click **OK**.

■ The new URL is added to the library.

WORK WITH SYMBOLS AND THE LIBRARY PANEL

You can use symbols stored in the Library panel to create new symbols or to duplicate symbols.

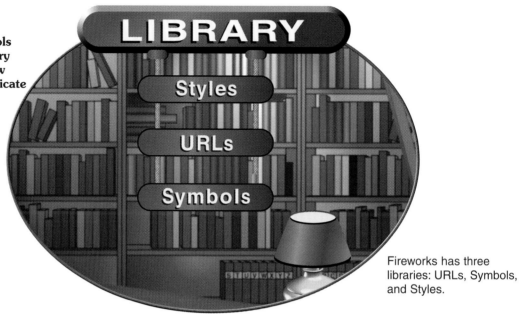

Fireworks has three libraries: URLs, Symbols, and Styles.

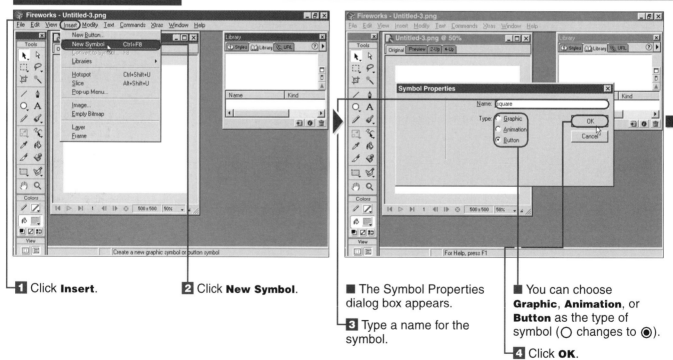

1 Click **Insert**.

2 Click **New Symbol**.

■ The Symbol Properties dialog box appears.

3 Type a name for the symbol.

■ You can choose **Graphic**, **Animation**, or **Button** as the type of symbol (○ changes to ◉).

4 Click **OK**.

After I create a symbol, does a copy of that symbol appear in the Library panel?

No. The original symbol appears in the Library panel and a copy, or instance, of the symbol appears in your document. Any copies you create from the Library panel are always instances. The original remains in the panel.

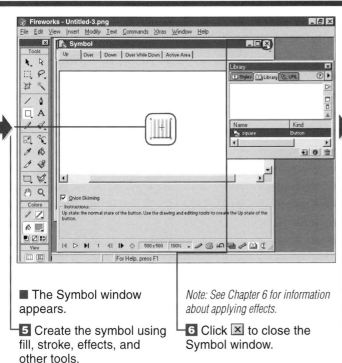

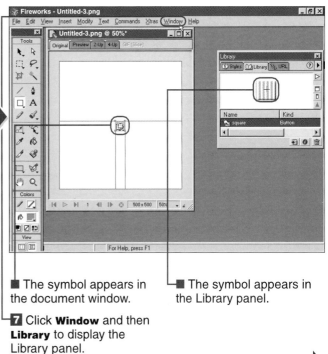

■ The Symbol window appears.

5 Create the symbol using fill, stroke, effects, and other tools.

Note: See Chapter 6 for information about applying effects.

6 Click ☒ to close the Symbol window.

■ The symbol appears in the document window.

7 Click **Window** and then **Library** to display the Library panel.

■ The symbol appears in the Library panel.

CONTINUED ➤

WORK WITH SYMBOLS AND THE LIBRARY PANEL

You can edit and duplicate the symbols in the library to use multiple copies of a symbol in your document.

DUPLICATE A SYMBOL

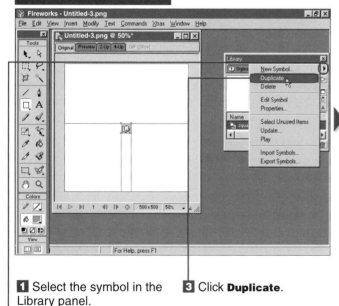

1 Select the symbol in the Library panel.

2 Click the Options ▶.

3 Click **Duplicate**.

4 Click and drag the symbol from the library to the document.

■ You can drag multiple copies to the document.

How can I edit one instance of the symbol but keep the other instances the same?

You can't: All instances are connected to the original, and any changes affect all copies. You can, however, insert a new symbol and format it as you like.

EDIT THE SYMBOL

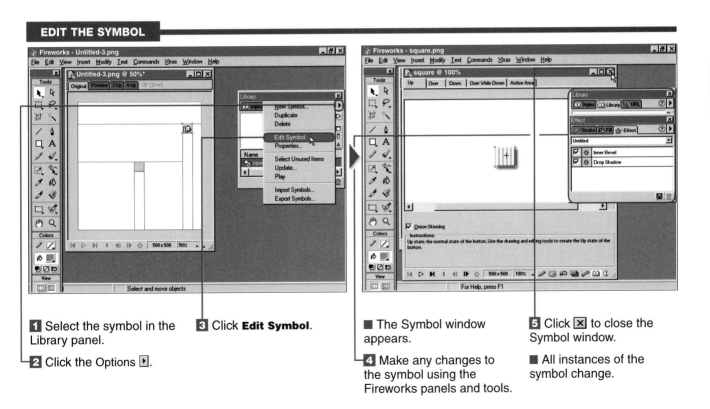

1 Select the symbol in the Library panel.

2 Click the Options ▶.

3 Click **Edit Symbol**.

■ The Symbol window appears.

4 Make any changes to the symbol using the Fireworks panels and tools.

5 Click ☒ to close the Symbol window.

■ All instances of the symbol change.

IMPORT AND UPDATE A BUTTON

You can import buttons from other documents to use in your current document. You update buttons when you make changes to the original.

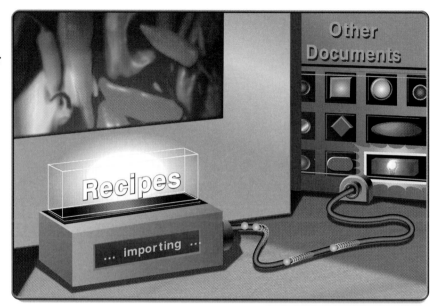

You can update and import graphic symbols and buttons.

IMPORT AND UPDATE A BUTTON

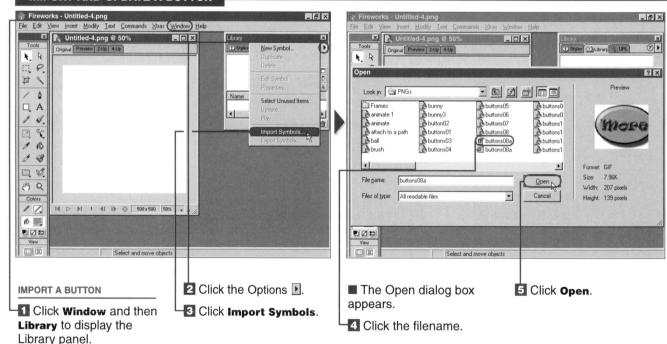

IMPORT A BUTTON

1 Click **Window** and then **Library** to display the Library panel.

2 Click the Options ▶.

3 Click **Import Symbols**.

■ The Open dialog box appears.

4 Click the filename.

5 Click **Open**.

Can I import symbols and graphics from other programs to Fireworks?

Yes. The Open dialog box displays all readable file types, including GIF, JPEG, BMP, and others.

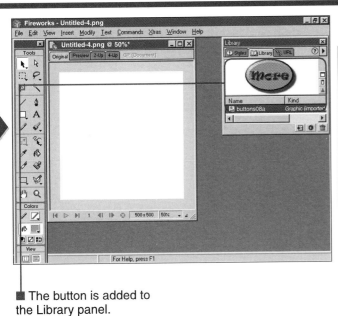

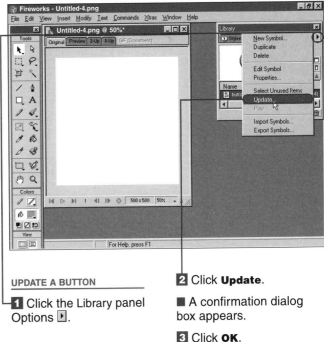

■ The button is added to the Library panel.

UPDATE A BUTTON

1 Click the Library panel Options ▸.

2 Click **Update**.

■ A confirmation dialog box appears.

3 Click **OK**.

CREATE A NAVIGATION BAR

You can create a navigation bar containing multiple buttons. Each button directs users to a different page on the Web site.

The buttons on a navigation bar use the same graphic design, but each displays different text.

CREATE A NAVIGATION BAR

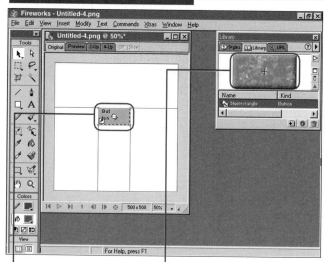

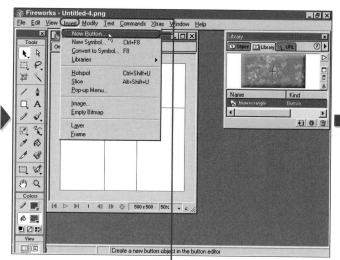

1 Create or import a button.

Note: For more information, see the sections "Create a Button" and "Import and Update a Button" earlier in this chapter.

Note: Do not add text to the new button yet.

■ The button appears in the Symbol library.

2 Move the original button to the side of the document.

■ The button symbol remains in the library.

3 Click **Insert**.

4 Click **New Button**.

Why do I keep the original button that has no text?

If you decide to change the graphic design of the button — fill, stroke, or effect — you can make changes to the original and choose that the changes be made to all instances.

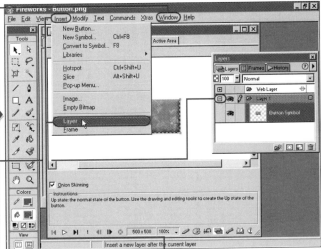

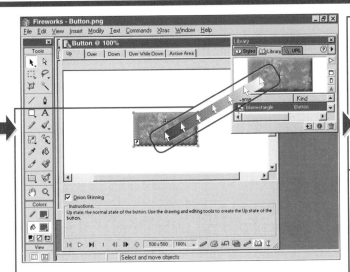

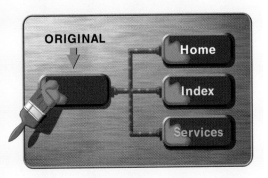

■ The Button Editor appears.

5 Click and drag the button from the Library panel to the Button Editor.

■ An instance of the button appears in the Button Editor.

Note: You can close the Library panel.

6 Click **Window** and then **Layers** to display the Layers panel.

■ You can close the Slice section of each layer by clicking ▣.

7 Click **Insert**.

8 Click **Layer**.

Note: For more information about layers, see Chapter 4.

CONTINUED ▶

CREATE A NAVIGATION BAR

All buttons on a navigation bar should use the same graphic design for consistency.

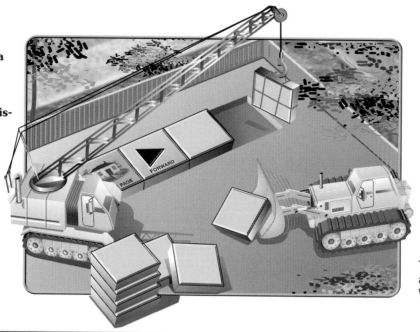

The same navigation bar appears on each of the Web pages in the site.

CREATE A NAVIGATION BAR (CONTINUED)

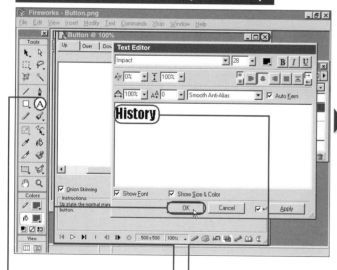

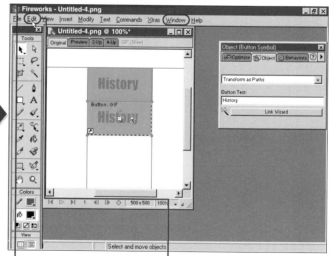

■ Layer 2 is automatically selected.

9 Click the Text tool (Ⓐ).

10 Click the button.

■ The Text Editor appears.

11 Type the text for the button.

12 Click **OK**.

13 Click ☒ to close the Button Editor.

■ You can click ☒ to close the Layers panel.

14 Click **Window** and then **Object** to display the Object panel.

15 Click **Edit** and then **Copy** to copy the button.

16 Click **Edit** and then **Paste** and move the copy off the top of the first button to paste the copy near the original button.

Can I edit a button after I create the navigation bar?

Yes. Double-click any button to edit it in the Button Editor. You have the choice of editing only the current button or all instances of the button.

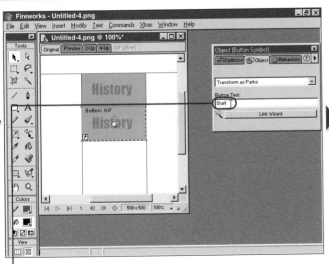

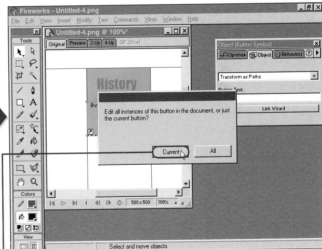

17 Type new next in the Button Text box for this button instance.

18 Press **Enter** (**Return**).

■ A confirmation dialog box appears.

19 Click **Current**.

■ Only the text for the current instance changes. Text on the other buttons remains the same.

*Note: You can repeat Steps **15** through **19** to add more buttons to the navigation bar.*

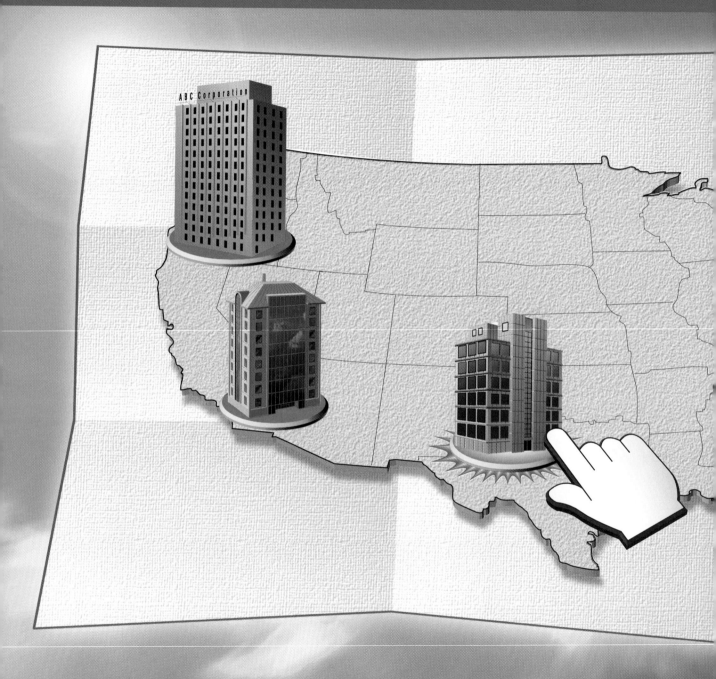

CHAPTER 8

Create Hotspots and Image Maps

Are you ready to link your buttons and images to other Web pages? This chapter can show you how to create hotspots and image maps.

UNDERSTAND HOTSPOTS AND IMAGE MAPS

You can use hotspots and image maps to help the site visitor navigate your Web site.

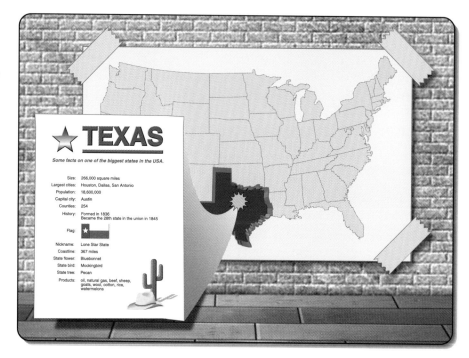

A *hotspot* is any part of a graphic or image that links to a URL. You can create hotspots in various shapes so that they conform to the shape of the graphic.

An *image map* is a graphic that contains multiple hotspots. Generally, an image map directs visitors to various pages within the site.

THE WEB LAYER

Fireworks places all hotspots on the Web layer. The Web layer, which is shared across all frames, can be hidden and locked.

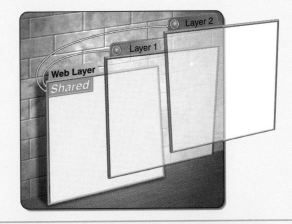

HOTSPOT TOOLS

With hotspot tools, you can draw a rectangle, square, circle, oval, or polygon shape. You can also convert an object to a hotspot, whether the object is a path, an image, or text.

IMAGE MAP FILES

An image map file contains the graphic plus multiple hotspots. The graphic can be a drawing, an image, text, or any combination of the three.

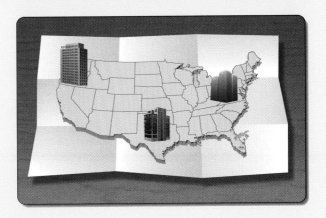

CREATE OR INSERT A HOTSPOT

You can create a hotspot on any graphic or text. Hotspots can link to another area of your Web page, or to a totally different Web page.

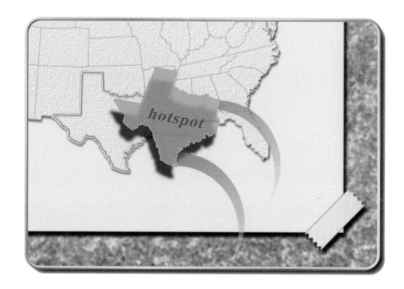

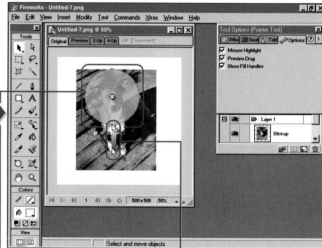

1 Click and hold the Hotspot tool (▢) and select the shape that you want to use.

Note: You can click ◯ to draw circle or oval shapes, ▢ to draw rectangles or squares, or ♡ to draw irregular shapes.

2 Draw the circle, rectangle, or polygon.

■ The hotspot shape appears over the graphic or image.

■ You can click a handle and drag to resize the hotspot shape.

What is the difference between creating and inserting a hotspot?

Generally, you create a circle or rectangle when you want only a portion of the image to act as a hotspot. You insert a hotspot when you want to use the entire image, graphic, or text instead of just a part of it. To learn more about creating text, objects, or images, see Chapters 3, 4, and 5.

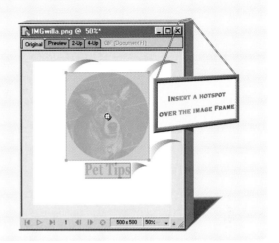

INSERT AND PREVIEW A HOTSPOT

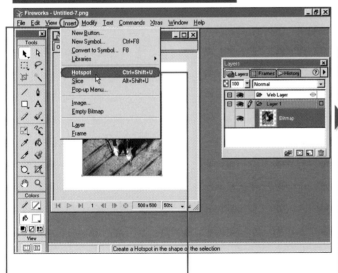

1 Select the graphic, text, or image that you want to insert as a hotspot.

2 Click **Insert**.

3 Click **Hotspot**.

■ The hotspot covers the entire graphic.

4 Click the **Preview** tab.

5 Drag ▷ over the graphic.

■ 🖑 indicates a hotspot.

EDIT HOTSPOTS

You can change or convert the shape of your hotspots to better fit an image or graphic. You can change a shape by altering the size of a rectangle or circle. You convert the shape when changing a rectangle to a circle, for example.

CHANGE THE SHAPE SIZE

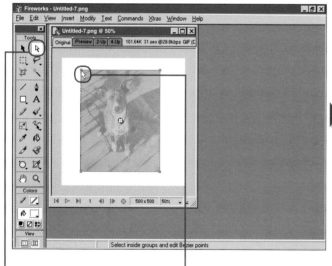

1 Click the Subselection tool (⬚).

2 Click any hotspot handle.

Note: Press and hold **Shift** *as you draw to form a perfect circle or square.*

3 Drag the handle to change the shape of the hotspot.

■ You can click and drag the hotspot shape to change its placement.

**Why would I want to change
the color of the hotspot?**

Changing the hotspot's color
changes only what you see
on-screen. It does not affect
how the hotspot works or
appears on the Web page.
You can change the color to
better distinguish between a
hotspot and a slice, for
example. For more information
about slices, see Chapter 9.

CONVERT THE SHAPE

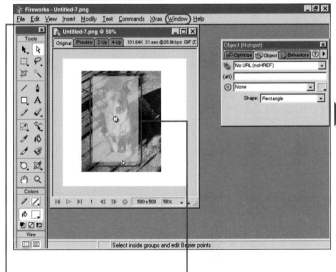

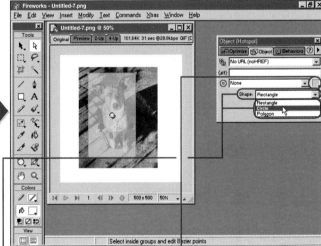

1 Click **Window** and then
Object to display the Object
panel.

2 Select the hotspot.

3 Click the Shape ⏷.

4 Click the shape you want
to convert to.

■ You can change the color
of the hotspot by clicking the
color swatch and choosing a
new color.

■ Fireworks converts the
shape of your hotspot.

CONTINUED

EDIT HOTSPOTS

You can scale, rotate, skew, or distort your hotspot to better define the shape of your graphic.

SCALE OR ROTATE A HOTSPOT

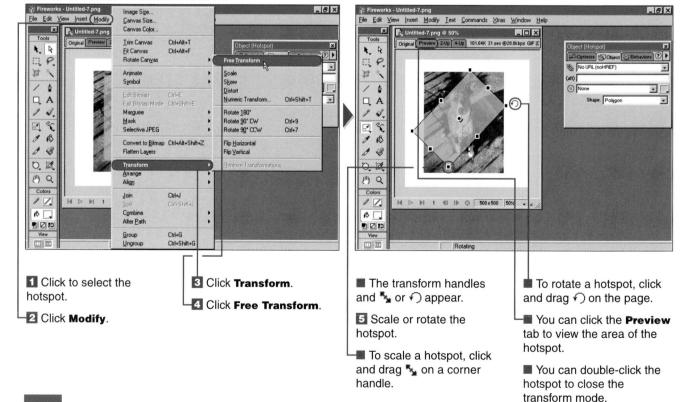

1 Click to select the hotspot.

2 Click **Modify**.

3 Click **Transform**.

4 Click **Free Transform**.

■ The transform handles and 🔺 or 🔁 appear.

5 Scale or rotate the hotspot.

■ To scale a hotspot, click and drag 🔺 on a corner handle.

■ To rotate a hotspot, click and drag 🔁 on the page.

■ You can click the **Preview** tab to view the area of the hotspot.

■ You can double-click the hotspot to close the transform mode.

Why would I need to transform a hotspot?

You might need to fit a hotspot to an unusual shape, such as a diamond or parallelogram. Tranforming a hotspot can help you do so: Scaling a hotspot changes its size, rotating a hotspot turns it around on the page, and skewing and distorting a hotspot enable you to change the size and shape of one or two sides.

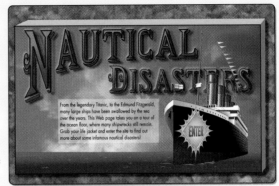

SKEW OR DISTORT A HOTSPOT

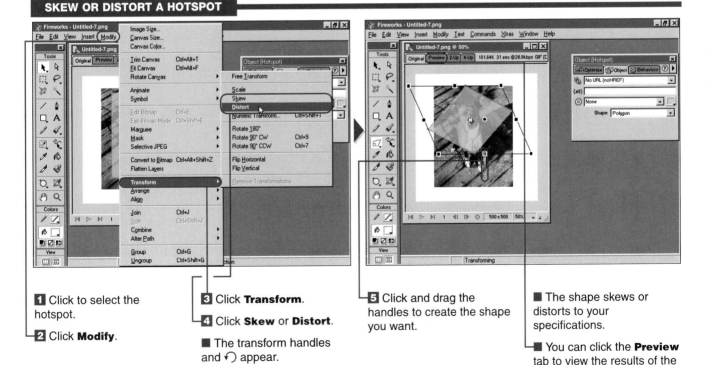

1 Click to select the hotspot.

2 Click **Modify**.

3 Click **Transform**.

4 Click **Skew** or **Distort**.

■ The transform handles and ⟲ appear.

5 Click and drag the handles to create the shape you want.

■ The shape skews or distorts to your specifications.

■ You can click the **Preview** tab to view the results of the transformed hotspot.

ASSIGN A URL TO A HOTSPOT

You can assign a URL to
a hotspot so that when
clicked, the hotspot
displays another Web
page.

Assigning a URL is the
same as linking the hotspot
to a Web page.

ASSIGN A URL TO A HOTSPOT

1 Select the hotspot.

2 Click **Window** and then
Object to display the Object
panel.

*Note: For more information about
URLs and the Object panel, see
Chapter 7.*

3 Type the URL.

4 Press Enter (Return).

*Note: You can enter multiple URLs.
For more information, see Chapter 7.*

What is a target?

A *target* defines the Web page window in which the linked file opens. _blank opens in a new window but keeps the old window available; _self opens in the same frame as the link; _parent opens in the parent frame; and _top opens in the same window as the current page, replacing any frames in the window.

_blank

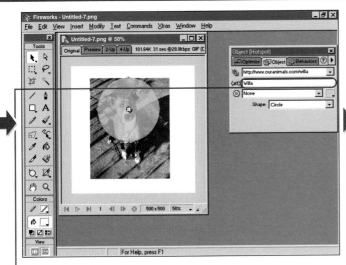

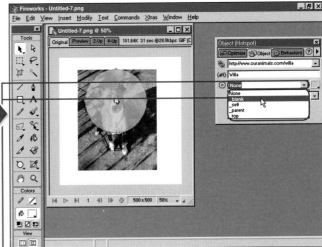

■ You can type alternate text.

Note: Alternate text appears when the cursor points to the image on the Web page.

5 Click the Link Target ⬇.

6 Click a target.

Note: You can click __blank__, __self__, __parent__, __top__, or __None__.

■ Fireworks assigns the URL to your hotspot.

CREATE AN IMAGE MAP

You can create an image map of your Web site that helps people navigate your site.

The image map contains links to other Web pages in the site.

1 Create the image, graphic, or text for your image map.

Note: For more on creating images, graphics, or text, see Chapters 3, 4, and 5.

2 Save the file.

Note: For more about saving a file, see Chapter 2.

3 Create hotspots (see the section "Create or Insert a Hotspot").

■ You can create circles, rectangles, or polygon hotspots.

Is there a limit to the number of hotspots I can use in an image map?

No, you can use as many hotspots as you like. You must remember, however, that the more hotspots you use, the larger the image map file becomes. Larger files take longer to download and open on the Web.

4 Double-click the hotspot.

■ The Object panel is displayed.

5 Click to select a hotspot.

6 Type the URL link.

■ You can type any alternate text.

7 Repeat Steps **4** through **6** for each hotspot.

■ You now have an image map.

Note: To learn how to export an image map, see Chapter 13.

ADD A POP-UP MENU

You can add a
pop-up menu to
any hotspot or
slice.

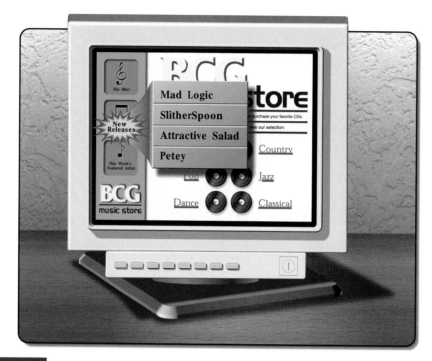

For more information
about slices, see
Chapter 9.

ADD A POP-UP MENU

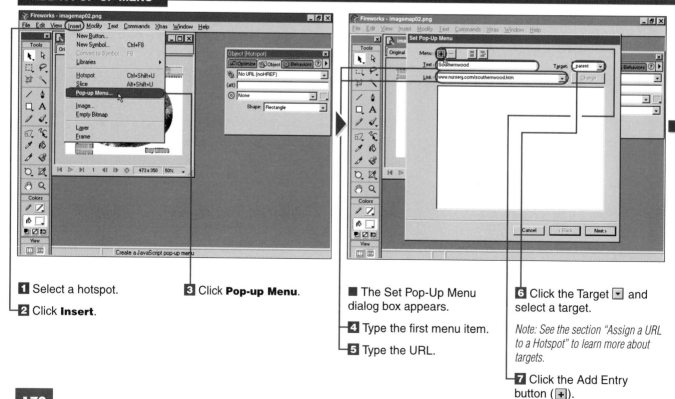

1 Select a hotspot.

2 Click **Insert**.

3 Click **Pop-up Menu**.

■ The Set Pop-Up Menu
dialog box appears.

4 Type the first menu item.

5 Type the URL.

6 Click the Target ▾ and
select a target.

*Note: See the section "Assign a URL
to a Hotspot" to learn more about
targets.*

7 Click the Add Entry
button (⊞).

What does a pop-up menu do?

A *pop-up menu* is similar to an image map. Each item on the menu contains a link to another Web page for quick and easy Web site navigation.

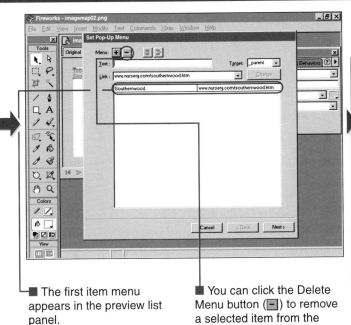

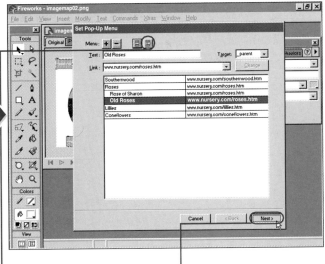

■ The first item menu appears in the preview list panel.

8 Repeat Steps **4** through **7** to add multiple menu items.

■ You can click the Delete Menu button (⊟) to remove a selected item from the preview list panel.

■ You can click the Indent Menu button (⊟) to indent menu items.

9 Click **Next**.

■ The second Set Pop-Up Menu dialog box appears.

CONTINUED ▶

ADD A POP-UP MENU

You can format the fonts and cells in a pop-up menu.

A *cell* refers to the background of the menu items.

ADD A POP-UP MENU (CONTINUED)

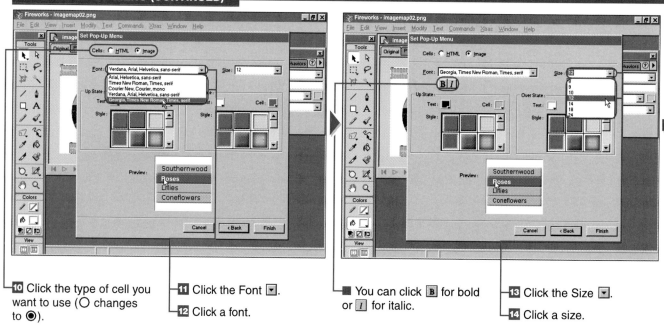

-10 Click the type of cell you want to use (O changes to ⊙).

-11 Click the Font ▾.

-12 Click a font.

■ You can click B for bold or I for italic.

-13 Click the Size ▾.

-14 Click a size.

What is the difference between HTML and Image cells?

HTML provides a flat look to the menu, whereas Image provides a three-dimensional look.

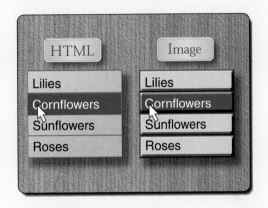

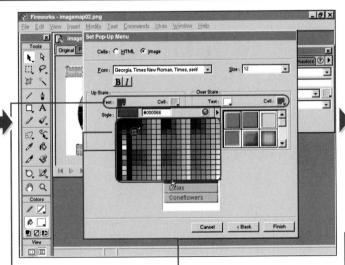

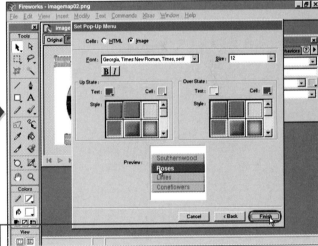

15 Select the text and cell color for the up and over states of your pop-up menu by clicking 🔽 in the Text and Cell boxes.

Note: The up state *shows the way the menu item normally looks on the Web page. The* over state *shows the*

way the menu looks when a cursor passes over the menu item.

■ A color palette appears for each.

16 Select the color you want.

Note: If you use cell images instead of HTML, choose the style for the up and over states.

17 Click **Finish**.

■ Fireworks adds a pop-up menu to your hotspot.

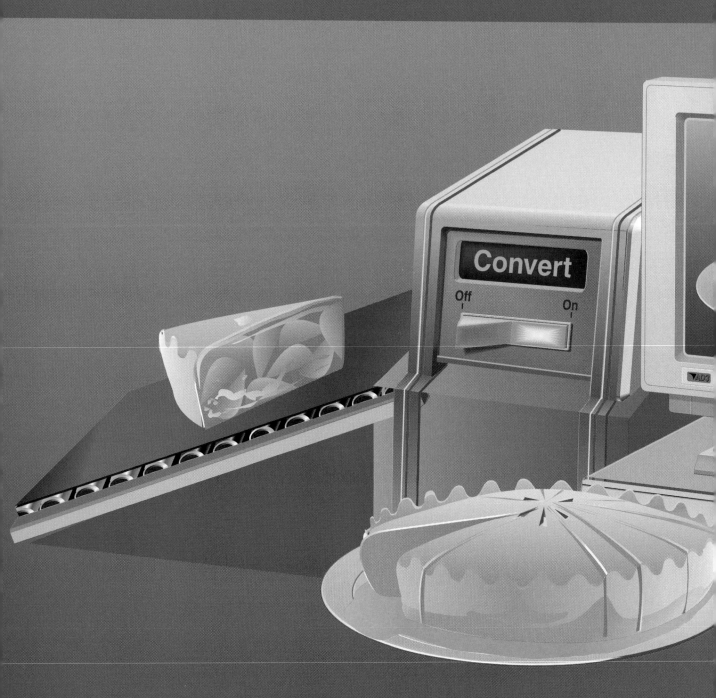

Slice Images

Are you wondering how you can make large image or graphic files load quickly? This chapter shows you how to slice files to help with download time.

UNDERSTAND SLICES

You can use slices to divide a graphic into smaller pieces, which download on your Web site more efficiently than an entire graphic file.

WHAT IS A SLICE?

A slice is one piece of a larger image, graphic, or text. You divide graphics into slices so that they load onto the Web page more quickly, and you can use a slice for animations and rollovers.

A SLICE ADVANTAGE

You can save each slice file in a different format. You might use JPEG for detailed image slices, for example, and GIF for less important areas of the graphic.

OTHER SLICE ADVANTAGES

You can link slices as you would a button or hotspot. You can also easily update slices, say if you want the date or a headline updated.

INTERACTIVE SLICES

You can use slices to create buttons, navigation bars, and rollovers. These slices respond when the mouse pointer passes over or clicks the slice.

SLICES AS WEB OBJECTS

Slices convert a graphic to HTML code and export the code to an HTML table on the Web page. The HTML code is reassembled to create each slice and then the entire graphic.

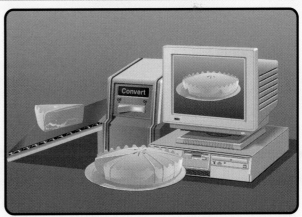

USING THE SLICE TOOLS

You can use the slice tools to create slices that are either rectangular or a polygon.

You cannot create slices that are circles or natural shapes.

CREATE A RECTANGULAR SLICE

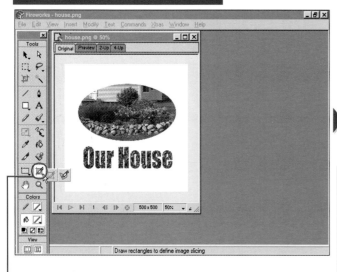

1 Click the Rectangle Slice tool (▨).

■ A box appears with tool shapes that you can select.

2 Draw the slice.

■ The cursor remains + until you click another tool.

■ The slice appears as a green rectangle.

What are the red lines around the slice?

As you draw a slice, Fireworks adds slice guides. You use the slice guides to help you align other slices and therefore keep the number of slice files to a minimum. Having fewer slices means that the image downloads quicker.

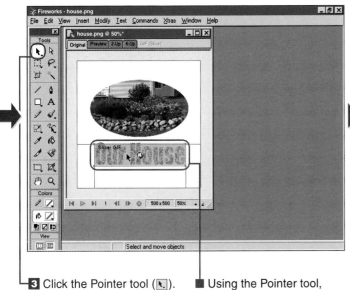

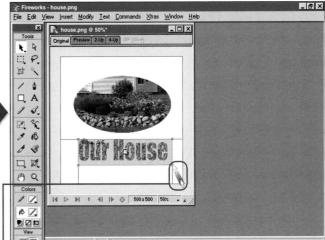

3 Click the Pointer tool ().

■ Using the Pointer tool, you can drag the slice around on the page to better cover the image.

4 Click and drag the corner handle to resize the slice.

Note: The slice should be as small as possible for optimum use.

CONTINUED

USING THE SLICE TOOLS

You can cut a polygon slice to make the slice smaller by outlining a shape that is not rectangular, such as an oval. Slicing only the image and not the background makes a more efficient and smaller slice.

CREATE A POLYGON SLICE

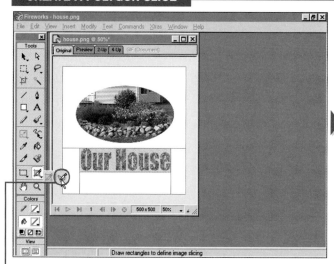

1 Click 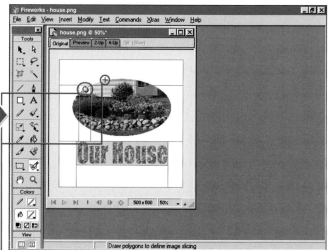 and select the Polygon Slice tool (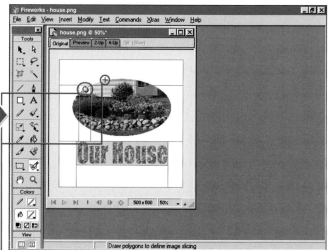) from the box that appears.

2 Click + where you want to begin the shape.

3 Click + at a second point.

■ Red guidelines appear.

■ The blue line is the slice shape.

How does Fireworks export a polygon slice?

Fireworks exports a polygon slice as a series of rectangles. A polygon slice often results in more individual files and takes longer to load on the browser. You should use a rectangle slice whenever possible to save space and time.

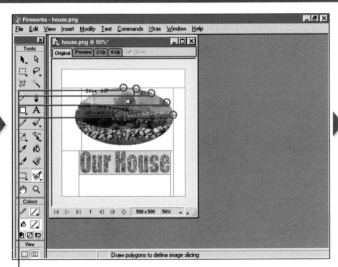

4 Continue to click + around the graphic.

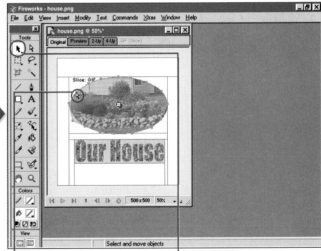

5 Click the tool on top of the first point to close the shape.

■ You are finished creating your polygon slice.

■ You can click 🔖 to adjust the slice on the object.

HIDE AND DISPLAY SLICE GUIDES

You can hide or display slice guides if you want to get them out of your way for a while as you are working.

Fireworks automatically creates guides as you draw a slice.

HIDE AND DISPLAY SLICE GUIDES

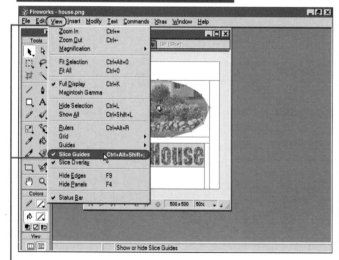

HIDE SLICE GUIDES

1 Click **View**.

2 Click **Slice Guides**.

■ The check mark disappears from in front of the command, and Fireworks hides the slice guides.

DISPLAY SLICE GUIDES

1 Click **View**.

2 Click **Slice Guides**.

■ A check mark appears in front of the command, and Fireworks displays the slice guides.

You can hide a slice so that you can view or edit an image or graphic more easily.

HIDE OR SHOW A SLICE

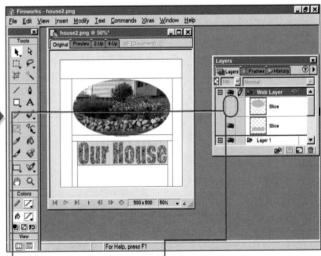

HIDE A SLICE

1 Select the slice.

2 Click **Window** and then **Layers** to display the Layers panel.

Note: Slices appear on the Web layer.

3 Click 👁.

■ The 👁 disappears, and Fireworks hides the slice.

REDISPLAY A SLICE

1 Click the 👁's now-empty box again.

■ The 👁 reappears, and Fireworks redisplays the slice.

Each slice must have a unique filename. Fireworks names all slices automatically.

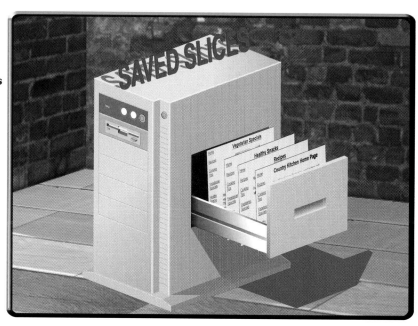

An example of a slice name is "image_r5_c3."

SLICE BASENAME

The slice basename is the name of the Fireworks document. In the example "image_r5_c3," *image* is the name of the Fireworks document.

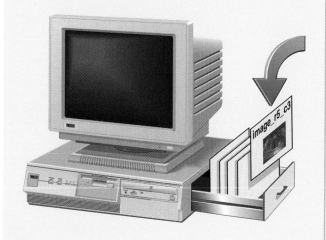

SLICE SUFFIX

Fireworks adds a suffix to the name that describes the slice's position in the HTML table. In the example "image_r5_c3," *r5* is row 5 and *c3* is column number 3.

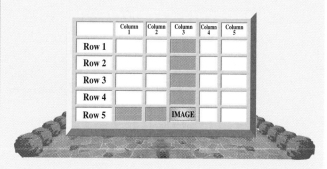

You can manually
name slices, to easily
locate an image
reference in the HTML
code.

TableObjects_r4_c3

NAME A SLICE

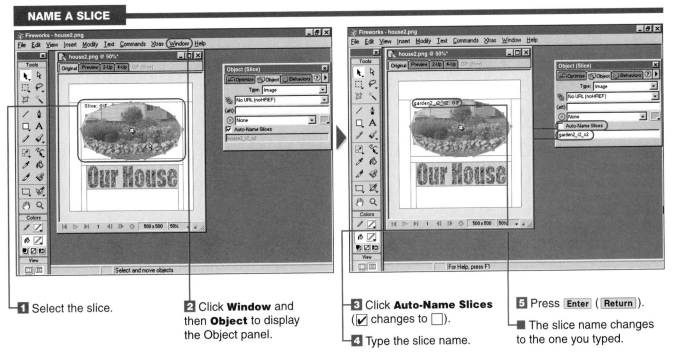

1 Select the slice.

2 Click **Window** and then **Object** to display the Object panel.

3 Click **Auto-Name Slices** (☑ changes to ☐).

4 Type the slice name.

5 Press **Enter** (**Return**).

■ The slice name changes to the one you typed.

CREATE A TEXT SLICE

You can use a text slice to display HTML text in the browser instead of an image.

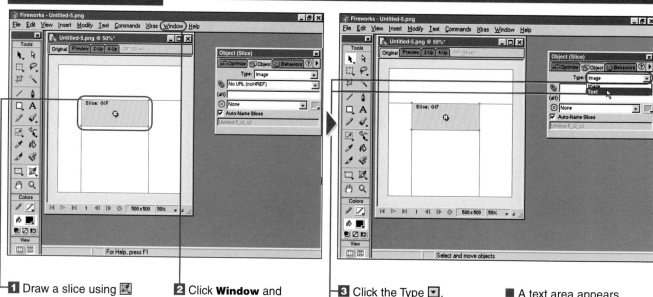

1 Draw a slice using ▨ (see the section "Using the Slice Tools").

2 Click **Window** and then **Object** to display the Object panel.

3 Click the Type ▾.

4 Click **Text**.

■ A text area appears in the Object panel.

When would I use text slices instead image slices?

You can use a text slice when you want to quickly update text on your Web site without having to create new graphics.

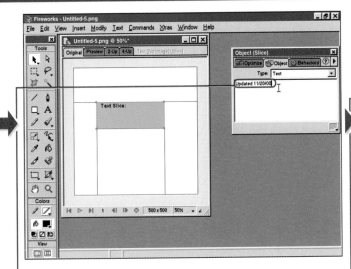

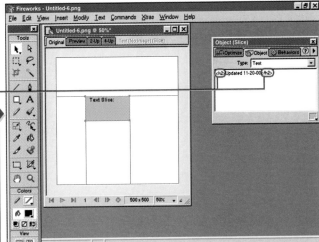

5 Type the text.

Note: The text in the slice does not appear in the Fireworks document. It does appear in a Web browser.

■ You can add HTML formatting tags to format the text.

Note: HTML text may look different when viewed in different browsers.

ASSIGN A URL LINK TO AN IMAGE SLICE

You can assign a
URL to any slice in
order to link it to
another Web page.

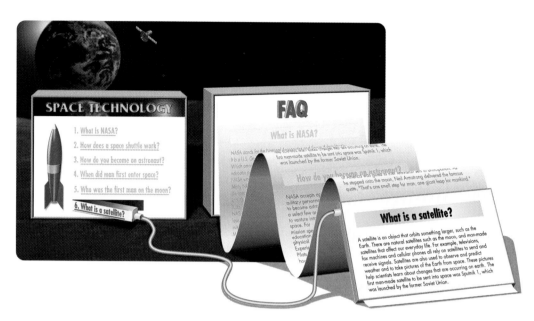

ASSIGN A URL LINK TO AN IMAGE SLICE

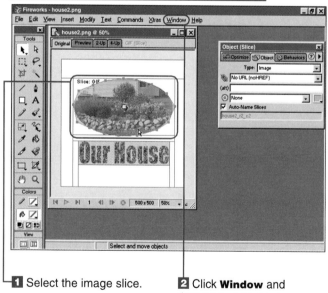

1 Select the image slice.

2 Click **Window** and then **Object** to display the Object panel.

3 Click the Current URL ▾.

4 Click the URL that you want to assign to the slice.

■ You can type the URL if it is not already in the list.

How do the URL lists in the URL Library panel and the Object panel differ?

The URL Library panel contains a list of URLs you might use in linking buttons, slices, and other graphics when you are working. In the Object panel, the URL text box describes the URL for only one object. The drop-down URL list in the Object panel comes from the URL Library. You can add URLs for use with all documents in the URL Library panel, but you can add URLs to the Object panel for use with only the current document.

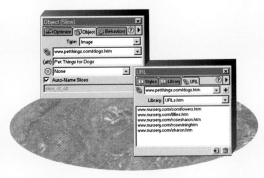

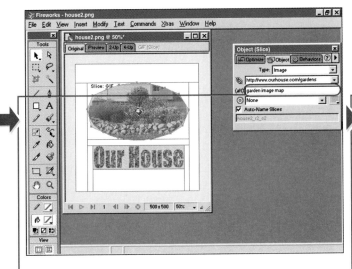

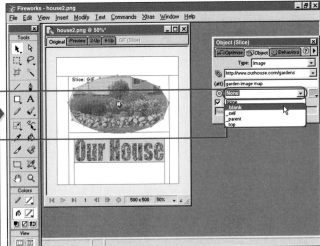

■ Optionally, type the alternate text.

Note: For information about alternate text, see Chapter 8.

5 Click the Link Target 🔽.

6 Click a link target.

Note: To learn about link targets, see Chapter 8.

■ The link target is assigned to your slice.

UPDATE AND EXPORT A SLICE

You can update and export a slice of an image or graphic instead of the entire image — for example, if you made changes to only one slice within the document.

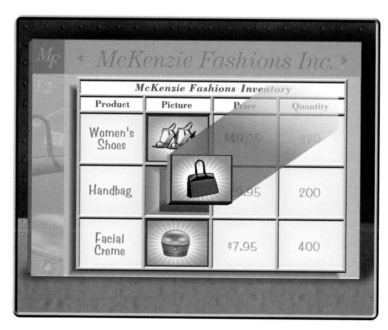

To learn about exporting slices, see Chapter 13.

UPDATE AND EXPORT A SLICE

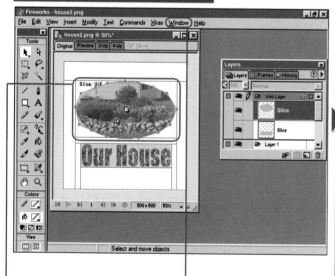

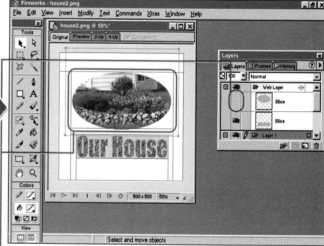

UPDATE THE SLICE

1 Select the slice.

2 Click **Window** and then **Layers** to display the Layers panel.

3 Click 👁 to hide the selected slice (👁 disappears).

4 Select the image or graphic.

5 Make changes to the graphic.

Note: For information about modifying images, see Chapter 5.

Why would I export a slice?

You export the slice to use in other applications, such as Dreamweaver or FrontPage. Before you export a slice, you need to optimize it first. Optimizing the slice compresses it and makes it load faster to the Web page. See Chapter 12 for information about optimizing graphics. See Chapter 13 for information about exporting graphics.

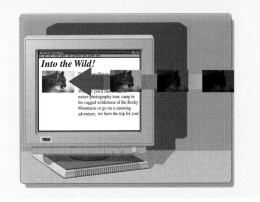

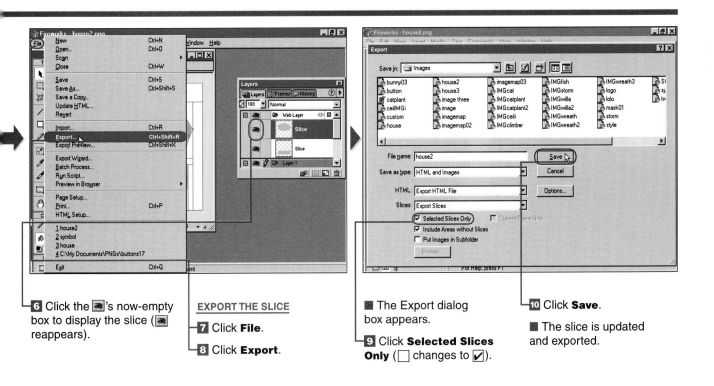

6 Click the 🖼's now-empty box to display the slice (🖼 reappears).

EXPORT THE SLICE

7 Click **File**.

8 Click **Export**.

■ The Export dialog box appears.

9 Click **Selected Slices Only** (☐ changes to ☑).

10 Click **Save**.

■ The slice is updated and exported.

ADJUST OVERLAPPING SLICES

You can rearrange slices in the stacking order so that one slice does not interfere with another.

Alternatively, you can redraw the overlapping slice.

ADJUST OVERLAPPING SLICES

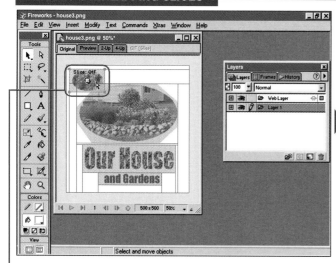

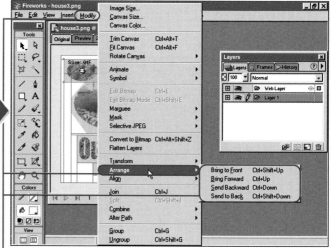

1 Select the underlying slice.

Note: It is better to use polygon slices in overlaps because of the way they cut slices for export. To learn more about polygon slices, see the section "Using the Slice Tools."

2 Click **Modify**.

3 Click **Arrange**.

4 Click **Bring to Front**, **Send to Back**, **Send Backward**, or **Bring Forward**.

Note: Each option moves the slice to another area within the stack.

■ The overlapping slice rearranges, depending on your selection.

Note: For information about arranging graphics, see Chapter 4.

You can assign interactivity to slices, such as rollovers and animations. Slices that perform some sort of action make the Web page more exciting and give the visitor more information.

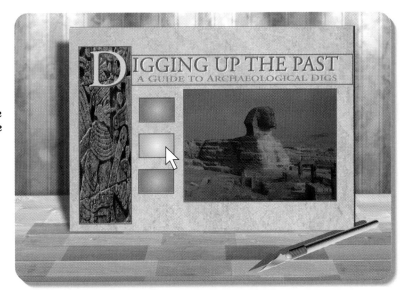

See Chapter 10 for more information about rollovers. See Chapter 11 for information about animations.

SLICES AND ROLLOVERS

A rollover is a graphic or image that changes appearance when the mouse cursor passes over it. You use slices to make rollovers interactive.

SLICES AND ANIMATIONS

Use slices to reduce the file size of animations and to animate specific areas of an image while the rest of the image remains static.

CHAPTER 10

Create Rollovers

Do you want to add interactivity to your Web pages? Do you want to involve the Web page visitor? This chapter shows you how with rollovers.

UNDERSTAND ROLLOVERS

A *rollover* is a graphic that changes appearance in the browser when the mouse pointer moves over or clicks the button.

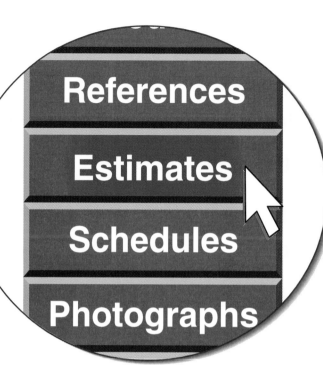

Fireworks rollovers include buttons, swapped images, and toggled images.

BUTTONS

A *button* is a graphic you create with the Button Editor. You can use up to four different states: Up, Down, Over, and Over While Down to create a rollover.

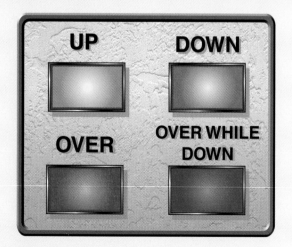

SWAPPED IMAGE ROLLOVER

A *swapped image rollover* exchanges the original image with another image from any frame you select when the cursor points to or clicks on the original image.

TOGGLED IMAGES

In a simple rollover, a *toggled image* changes when the pointer passes over or clicks the image. Toggled images swap the image from one specific frame only. For more information about frames, see Chapter 11.

DISJOINT ROLLOVER

A *disjoint rollover* changes the area that is not under the cursor. For example, when the cursor points to an image, text may appear beside the image.

Stonehenge, one of the world's most enduring mysteries, is located near Bath, England.

SLICES AND HOTSPOTS

Slices and hotspots are two foundations for creating rollovers in Fireworks. You use *slices* to make image or text files smaller by dividing them into pieces. *Hotspots* are small areas of an image or text that trigger an action on the Web page. For more information, see Chapters 8 and 9.

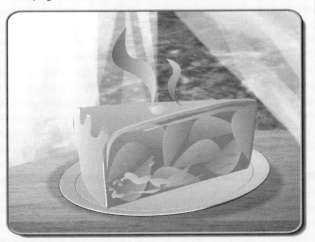

URL LINKS

You can link a URL to any rollover just as you link a URL to a hotspot or a slice. See Chapters 8 and 9 for more information.

UNDERSTAND BEHAVIORS

You can use behaviors to make a Web page interactive. You can use behaviors to create rollovers, hover buttons, image maps, and navigation bars, for example.

WHAT IS A BEHAVIOR?

A *behavior* is the action and reaction of an object in Fireworks and consists of an event and an action. An *event* such as clicking a button is the trigger that starts the action. An *action* is the result of the trigger, such as opening a browser window.

THE BEHAVIOR PANEL

You can write a programming code called *JavaScript* to define behaviors. Or with Fireworks, you can easily define behaviors for any image or button in the Behavior panel without writing JavaScript code.

HOTSPOTS AND SLICES

You assign behaviors to hotspots and slices differently in Fireworks. Hotspots are used only as triggers. Hotspots cannot perform an action. Slices, on the other hand, can trigger and receive events. For more information on hotspots and slices, see Chapters 8 and 9.

ATTACHED BEHAVIORS

Behaviors are attached to elements on a Web page, such as a text link or image. In Fireworks, you can also attach behaviors to slices or hotspots.

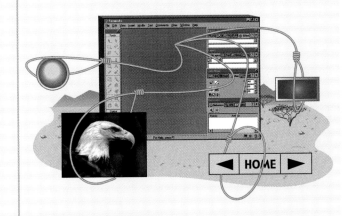

USING FRAMES

You must create multiple images or graphics to create a rollover effect. Each image or graphic resides in its own frame. For information about frames, see Chapter 11.

BEHAVIOR TYPES

Rollovers and image swaps are simple behaviors. Fireworks also lets you perform other behaviors, such as displaying text in the status bar of the browser window.

UNDERSTAND BEHAVIORS

Fireworks lets you create eight behaviors for your objects.
Each behavior acts and reacts differently.

SIMPLE ROLLOVER BEHAVIOR

A *simple rollover behavior* creates a rollover using two frames — one for the Up state and one for the Over state.

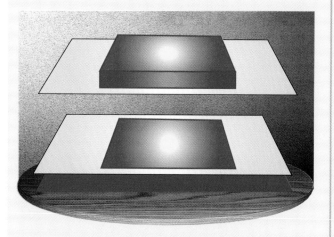

SWAP IMAGE BEHAVIOR

The *swap image behavior* uses one slice to replace another. The slices might be images, graphics, or text. See the section "Swap an Image" for more information.

SWAP IMAGE RESTORE BEHAVIOR

The *swap image restore behavior* returns the rollover to the image in Frame 1; it restores the original image.

SET NAV BAR IMAGE BEHAVIOR

The set nav bar image behavior is applied to each button in a navigation bar. The behavior sets each button to a specific state so that the navigation bar contains different buttons leading to different linked pages. See the section "Create a Disjoint Rollover" for more information.

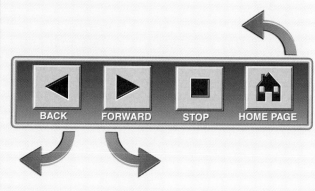

NAV BAR OVER BEHAVIOR

The nav bar over behavior sets the Over state for the slice that is a part of a navigation bar so that when the cursor passes over a button, the button displays differently than when the mouse clicks the button.

HOME PAGE

NAV BAR DOWN BEHAVIOR

The nav bar down behavior sets the Down state for the currently selected slice that is a part of a navigation bar. The Down state is displayed when you click the button.

FORWARD

NAV BAR RESTORE BEHAVIOR

The nav bar restore behavior reverts all slices on the navigation bar to their Up state. You use this behavior to return the navigation bar to its original state after it has been clicked.

SET TEXT OF STATUS BAR BEHAVIOR

The set text of status bar behavior lets you specify text that shows in the status bar of the browser window. The text that appears when you pass the cursor over a button, for example, can explain what happens when you click the button, such as taking you to another Web page.

CREATE A SIMPLE ROLLOVER

You can create
a button or
navigation bar that
uses a rollover
effect by using the
Button Editor.

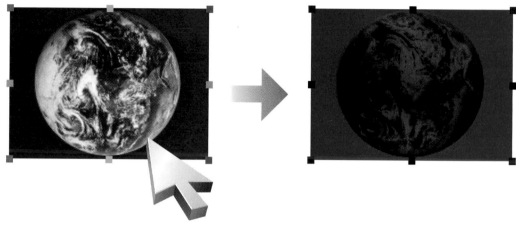

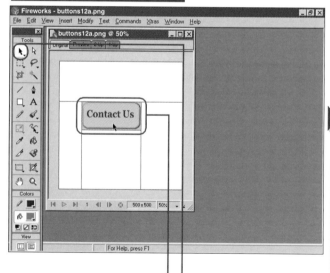

1 Open an existing button
document or create a new
one.

*Note: See Chapter 7 for information
about creating a new button.*

2 Click the Pointer tool (![pointer]).

3 Double-click the button.

■ The Button Editor
appears.

*Note: See Chapter 7 for more
information about the Button Editor.*

4 Click the **Over** tab.

5 Click **Copy Up Graphic**.

6 Click **Window** and then
Effect to display the Effect
panel.

7 Use the Effect panel to
edit the button for that state.

*Note: For information about the Up
and Down states, see Chapter 7.*

Can I use only effects to change the button in each state?

If you change the fill or stroke in one instance, that fill or stroke copies to all instances. However, you can add a new shape, button, text, or image.

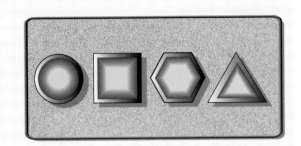

CREATE THE OVER WHILE DOWN STATE

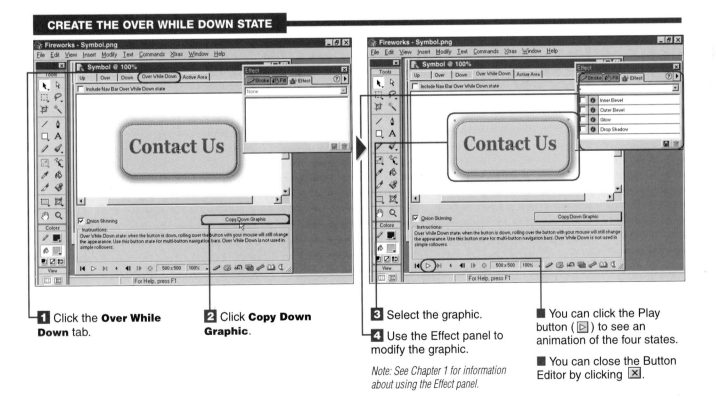

1 Click the **Over While Down** tab.

2 Click **Copy Down Graphic**.

3 Select the graphic.

4 Use the Effect panel to modify the graphic.

Note: See Chapter 1 for information about using the Effect panel.

■ You can click the Play button (▷) to see an animation of the four states.

■ You can close the Button Editor by clicking ☒.

DEFINE THE ACTIVE AREA

You can define the area of the graphic or image that is active. The *active area* is the area to which the mouse cursor must point to trigger the rollover.

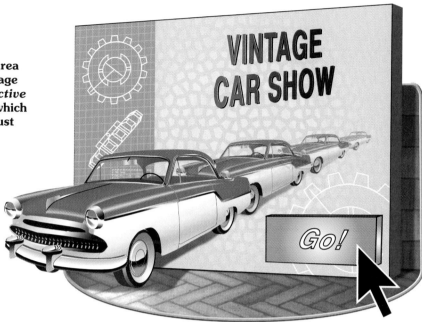

DEFINE THE ACTIVE AREA

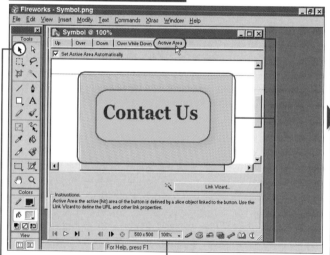

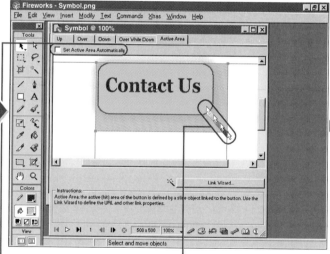

DEFINE THE AREA

1 Open an existing button document or create a new one.

Note: See Chapter 7 for information about creating a new button.

2 Click [cursor icon].

3 Double-click the button.

■ The Button Editor appears.

4 Click the **Active Area** tab.

■ The sliced area appears over the button.

5 Click **Set Active Area Automatically** (☑ changes to ☐).

6 Click and drag the slice handles to define the active area.

206

Do I have to set the active area?

No. Fireworks automatically sets a slice large enough to cover all states of the button. You can, however, change the size of the slice if you want.

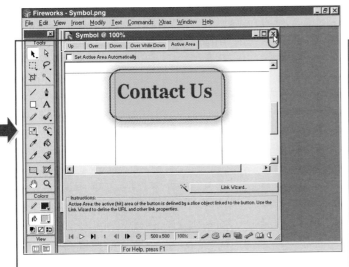

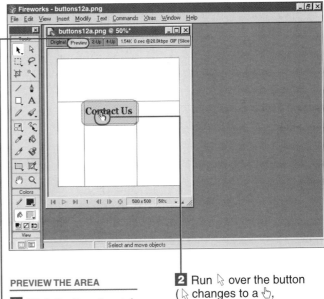

7 Click ⊠ to close the Button Editor.

■ The new slice appears in the document window.

PREVIEW THE AREA

1 Click the **Preview** tab.

2 Run ▷ over the button (▷ changes to a ⤴, indicating the active area).

ASSIGN A BEHAVIOR

You can apply a behavior
to a hotspot or a slice to
create rollovers and
other actions.

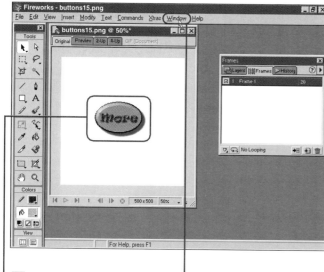

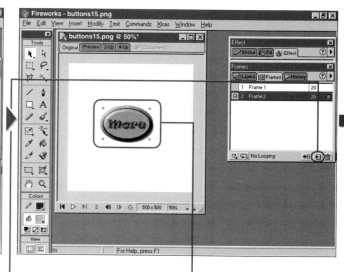

1 Create the graphic.

*Note: See Chapter 4 for more on
creating graphics.*

2 Click **Window** and then
Frames to display the
Frames panel.

*Note: For information about using
frames, see Chapter 11.*

3 Click the New/Duplicate
Frame button (⊞).

4 Create a graphic in the
second frame.

How can I create a second graphic that is similar to the first?

You can copy the original graphic. Then create a new frame and paste the graphic in that frame. You can then change the effect on either button. For more information about applying effects, see Chapter 6.

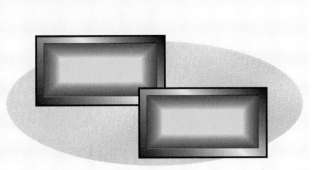

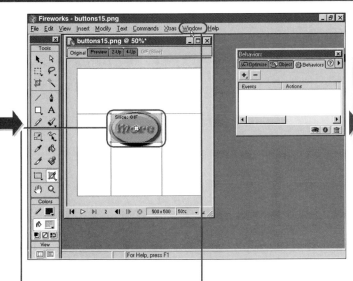

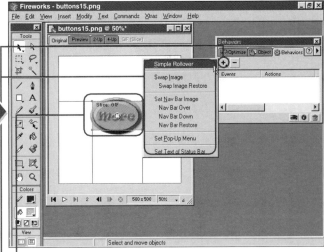

5 Insert a hotspot or slice on the graphic.

Note: For information about hotspots and slices, see Chapters 8 and 9.

6 Click **Window** and then **Behaviors** to display the Behaviors panel.

7 Select the hotspot or slice.

8 Click the Add Action button (⊞).

9 Click a behavior.

Note: Depending on the behavior you select, you may need to define the behavior further in a related dialog box.

■ Fireworks assigns the behavior to your graphic.

■ You can preview the rollover by clicking the **Preview** tab and then clicking ▷.

SWAP AN IMAGE

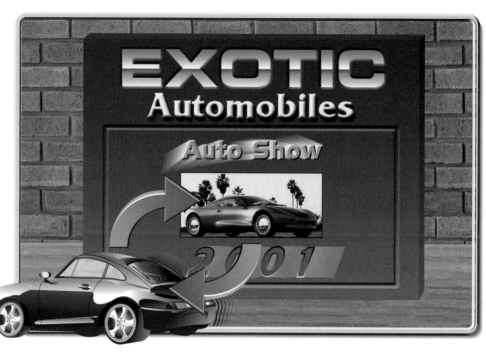

Using slices and behaviors, you can swap two images on your Web pages in response to the cursor's movement. When you pass the cursor over one image, another image appears. When you remove the cursor, the original image returns.

SWAP AN IMAGE

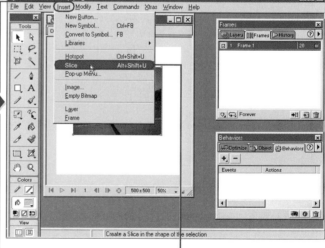

INSERT AN IMAGE

1 Insert an image.

Note: See Chapter 5 for information about inserting an image.

2 Select the image.

3 Click **Window** and then **Frames** to display the Frames panel.

4 Click **Window** and then **Behaviors** to display the Behaviors panel.

INSERT A SLICE OVER THE IMAGE

5 Click **Insert**.

6 Click **Slice**.

■ You can resize the slice if you want.

Note: For information about slices, see Chapter 9.

Should I create a larger slice or a smaller one for a rollover?

A large slice gives the Web visitor more area on which to click, and is therefore easier to see and use. However, large slices create larger files and take longer to load onto the page. Use a medium slice when in doubt.

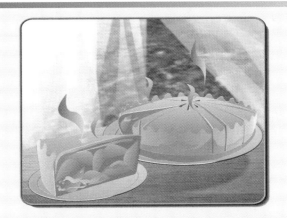

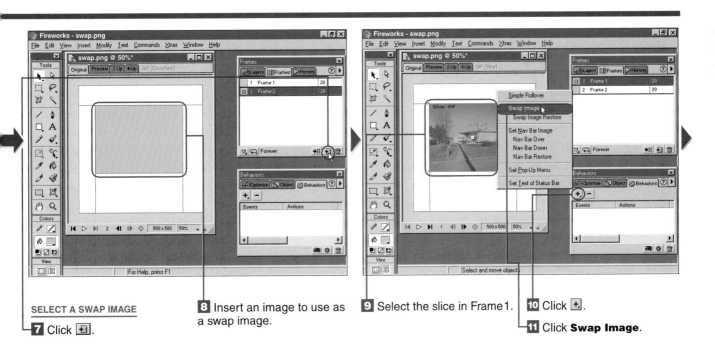

SELECT A SWAP IMAGE

7 Click 🗷.

8 Insert an image to use as a swap image.

9 Select the slice in Frame1.

10 Click 🗷.

11 Click **Swap Image**.

CONTINUED ▶

211

SWAP AN IMAGE

You can choose which image Fireworks swaps with the original image, so you can try several swaps on your Web page.

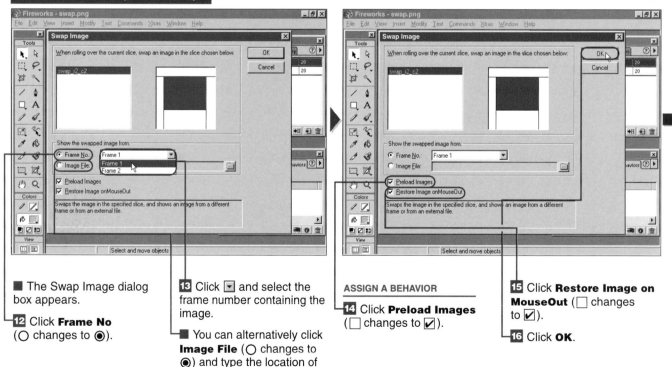

■ The Swap Image dialog box appears.

12 Click **Frame No** (○ changes to ◉).

13 Click ▼ and select the frame number containing the image.

■ You can alternatively click **Image File** (○ changes to ◉) and type the location of an image file to swap.

ASSIGN A BEHAVIOR

14 Click **Preload Images** (☐ changes to ☑).

15 Click **Restore Image on MouseOut** (☐ changes to ☑).

16 Click **OK**.

What do the Preload Images and Restore Image onMouseOut check boxes do?

Preload Images loads both images when the Web visitor opens the Web page. Restore Image onMouseOut restores the first image when you move the cursor away from the image. Preload Images guarantees that there is no delay in loading the image during the mouseover.

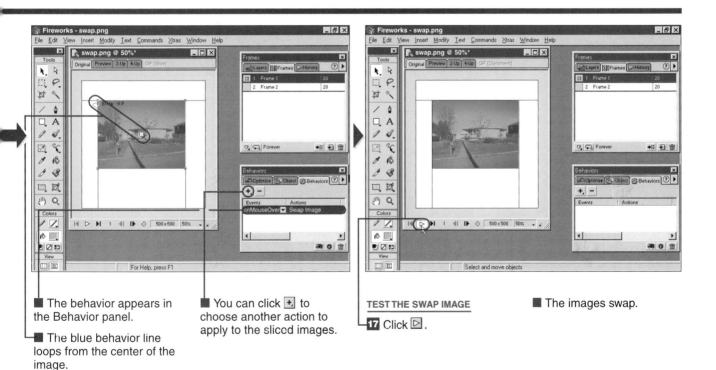

■ The behavior appears in the Behavior panel.

■ The blue behavior line loops from the center of the image.

■ You can click ➕ to choose another action to apply to the sliced images.

TEST THE SWAP IMAGE

17 Click ▷.

■ The images swap.

CREATE A DISJOINT ROLLOVER

You can create a disjoint rollover that displays an image on-screen when the cursor passes over the trigger anywhere else on the page.

Each image or graphic resides in its own frame and each requires its own slice.

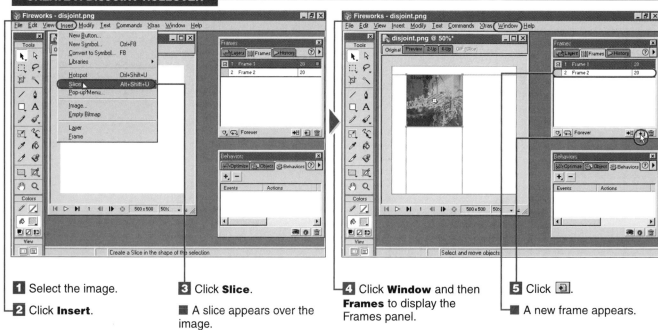

1 Select the image.

2 Click **Insert**.

3 Click **Slice**.

■ A slice appears over the image.

4 Click **Window** and then **Frames** to display the Frames panel.

5 Click 🔲.

■ A new frame appears.

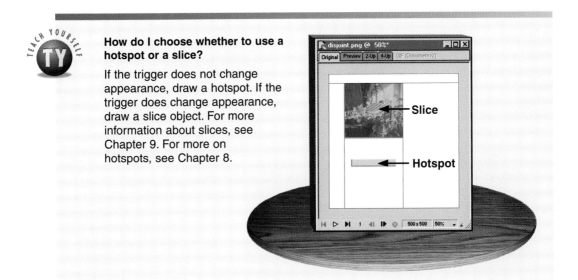

How do I choose whether to use a hotspot or a slice?

If the trigger does not change appearance, draw a hotspot. If the trigger does change appearance, draw a slice object. For more information about slices, see Chapter 9. For more on hotspots, see Chapter 8.

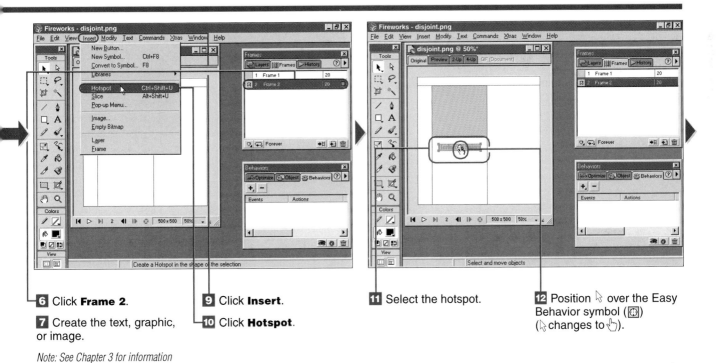

6 Click **Frame 2**.

7 Create the text, graphic, or image.

Note: See Chapter 3 for information about creating text.

8 Select the text.

9 Click **Insert**.

10 Click **Hotspot**.

11 Select the hotspot.

12 Position ⊿ over the Easy Behavior symbol (⊞) (⊿ changes to 🖑).

CONTINUED

CREATE A DISJOINT ROLLOVER

You can use the Easy Behavior symbol to create quick disjoint rollovers to liven up your Web page.

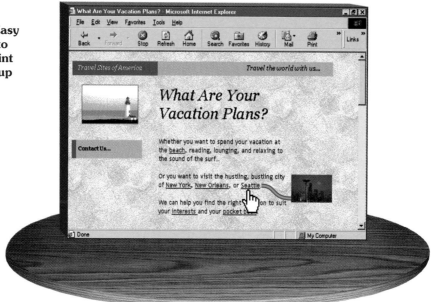

CREATE A DISJOINT ROLLOVER (CONTINUED)

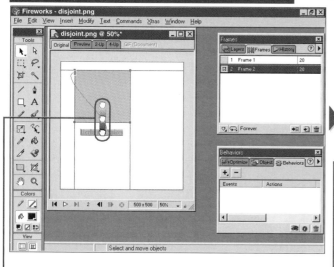

13 Click and drag ⊞ (🖑 changes to 🖑) to the slice covering the image.

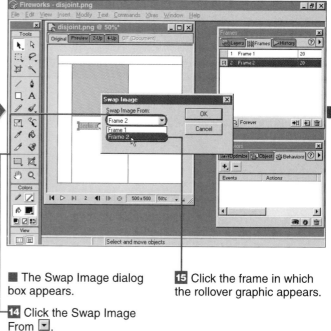

■ The Swap Image dialog box appears.

14 Click the Swap Image From ▾.

15 Click the frame in which the rollover graphic appears.

**Can I create a disjoint
rollover using a button as
the trigger?**

Yes. Create the button as you
normally would in the Button
Editor. Then attach the
behavior the same way you
do with a hotspot or slice.

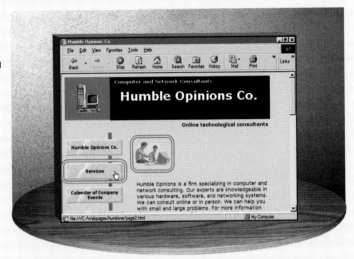

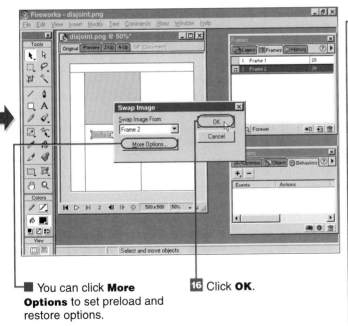

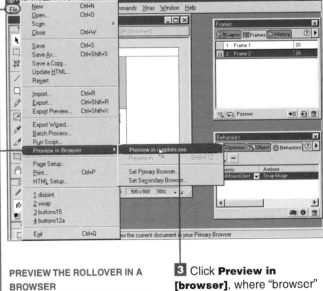

■ You can click **More
Options** to set preload and
restore options.

🔢16 Click **OK**.

**PREVIEW THE ROLLOVER IN A
BROWSER**

1️⃣ Click **File**.

2️⃣ Click **Preview in
Browser**.

3️⃣ Click **Preview in
[browser]**, where "browser"
is the primary browser on
your system.

■ The disjointed rollover
appears in your browser.

CHAPTER 11

Create Animations

Are you ready to have some fun with animations? This chapter shows you how to create animations in Fireworks.

UNDERSTAND ANIMATIONS

Using Fireworks animations, you can create banner ads, logos, and cartoons that move across a Web page.

FRAMES

You use one frame for each copy of a graphic and then change each copy slightly. You play the frames back like a movie to create the illusion of motion in the animation.

LAYERS

You can create different layers for each frame so that you have some static objects and other objects that move in the frame.

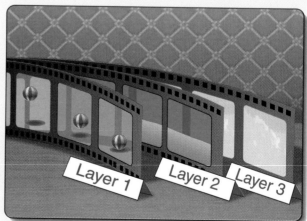

ANIMATION FILE FORMAT

Fireworks supports various
animation file types, such as
Animated GIF, Dynamic HTML,
Flash SWF, and JavaScript. Each
format has its advantages and
disadvantages. JavaScript lets
you use sound, for example, and
DHTML does not.

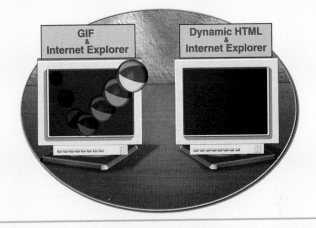

ANIMATED GIF FILES

You can use animated GIF as the
file format to save animations of
graphics and text. You can view
animated GIF files in more
browsers and platforms than many
other file types, even though it
offers no sound and fewer colors
than other formats.

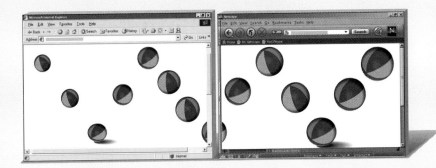

LOAD TIME

You can save your viewer
frustration by considering the time
it takes for the elements on your
Web page to load. Make your
animations short and concise.
Limit the number of colors, the
number of frames, and the
animated area.

MANAGE FRAMES

You can add and copy frames to a document so that you can add movement to an animation.

MANAGE FRAMES

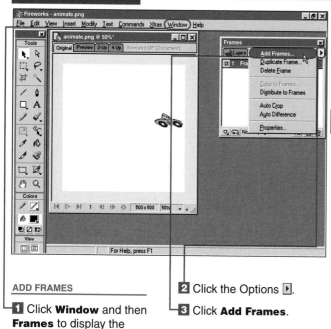

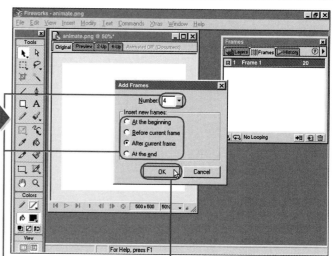

ADD FRAMES

1 Click **Window** and then **Frames** to display the Frames panel.

2 Click the Options ▶.

3 Click **Add Frames**.

■ The Add Frames dialog box appears.

4 Type the number of frames that you want to add.

5 Click to choose where to insert the new frames (○ changes to ⊙).

6 Click **OK**.

■ Fireworks adds the frames to the document window and Frames panel.

How many frames should I add for an animation?

The number of frames you add depends on your animation. You can guess at the number and then add or delete frames later as needed. You can also create two frames — one for the first animation and one for the last — and then fill in between the two by adding frames as you need them.

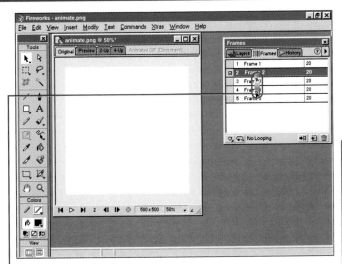

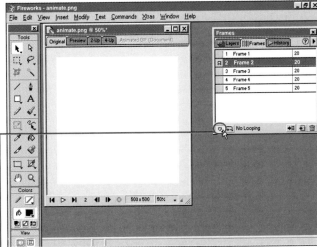

MOVE FRAMES

1 Click and drag the frame you want to move up or down to a new position.

■ The frame moves to its new position, and Fireworks renumbers the frames so that they are still in order.

VIEW FRAMES

1 Click the Onion Skinning button (⬚).

■ A pop-up menu appears.

2 Click the frames that you want to view.

■ Objects in other frames appear dimmed in the current frame.

CONTINUED

MANAGE FRAMES

You can copy and delete
frames to make your
animation flow more
smoothly.

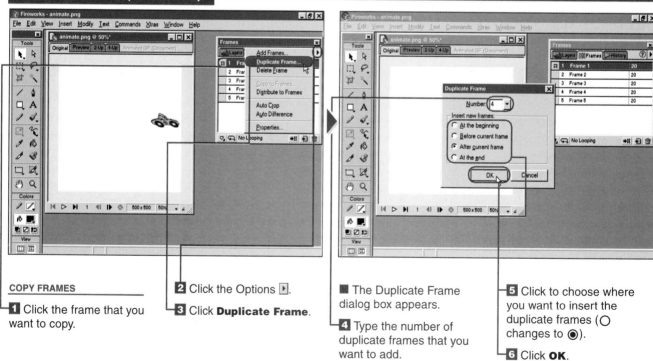

COPY FRAMES

1 Click the frame that you
want to copy.

2 Click the Options ▶.

3 Click **Duplicate Frame**.

■ The Duplicate Frame
dialog box appears.

4 Type the number of
duplicate frames that you
want to add.

5 Click to choose where
you want to insert the
duplicate frames (○
changes to ⦿).

6 Click **OK**.

■ Fireworks inserts the
frames.

What is the difference between adding a frame and duplicating a frame?

When you duplicate a frame, you also duplicate the graphic within the frame. When you add a frame, you add a blank frame.

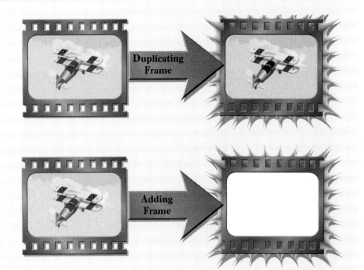

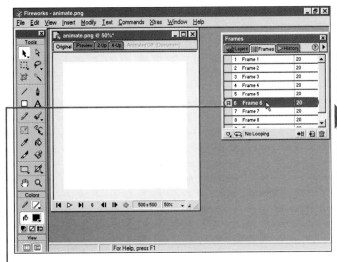

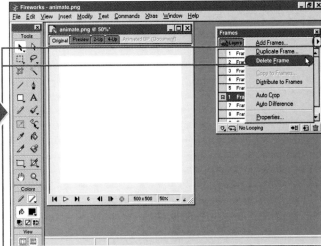

DELETE FRAMES

1 Click the frame in the Frames panel.

■ You can hold Shift and click two or more frames to delete multiple frames at one time.

2 Click the Options ▶.

3 Click **Delete Frame**.

■ Fireworks deletes the frame.

ANIMATE OBJECTS BY COPYING AND DISTRIBUTING OBJECTS IN FRAMES

You can copy and distribute objects so that the objects appear to be moving. You can change the position of each copy in a frame to simulate movement.

COPY TO FRAMES

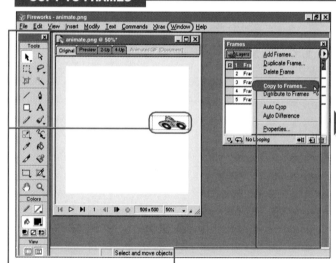

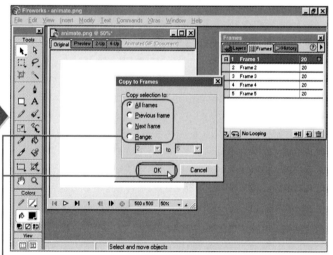

-1 Click **Window** and then **Frames** to display the Frames panel.

-2 Select the object.

-3 Click the Options ▶.

-4 Click **Copy to Frames**.

■ The Copy to Frames dialog box appears.

-5 Click the frames to which you want to copy the selected object.

-6 Click **OK**.

■ Fireworks copies the object to the selected frames.

-7 After you copy the graphic to the frames, move the object slightly in each frame to create an animation effect.

Note: See Chapter 4 for more on moving objects.

Why distribute objects to frames?

Distributing objects to frames is a fast way to create an animation from a static document. Distributing objects places each object in your document in a separate frame by itself according to the order in which you drew the objects.

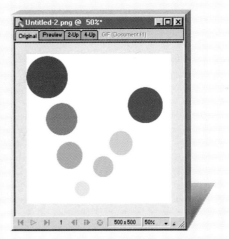

DISTRIBUTE OBJECTS TO FRAMES

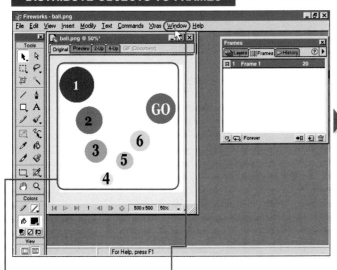

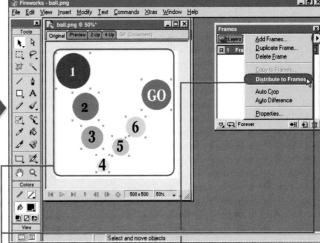

1 Create one or more objects in the first frame of the document.

Note: For more information about creating objects, see Chapter 4.

Note: You can group objects that will appear in the same frame (see Chapter 4).

2 Click **Window** and then **Frames** to display the Frames panel.

3 Select all the objects that you want to distribute.

■ You can press and hold the **Shift** key to select multiple objects.

4 Click the Options ▶.

5 Click **Distribute to Frames**.

■ Fireworks distributes your objects to different frames.

Note: See "Preview an Animation" for information about playing the animation.

SHARE LAYERS FOR STATIC OBJECTS

You can create background objects that you share among all frames. You have to create static objects only once. A *static object* is one that remains the same on every frame, without showing movement.

SHARE LAYERS FOR STATIC OBJECTS

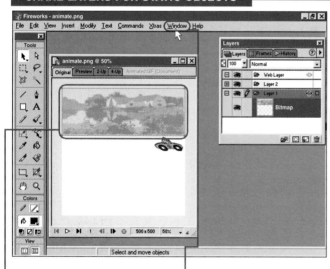

1 Create the background graphic or image.

Note: For information about creating graphics or images, see Chapters 4 and 5.

2 Click **Window** and then **Layers** to display the Layers panel.

3 Double-click the layer that you want to share.

■ The Layer Name dialog box appears.

**On which layer do I draw
my animated graphics?**

All frames share any
object on Layer 1. If the
background object is on
Layer 1, you must draw
animated graphics on
Layer 2 or 3.

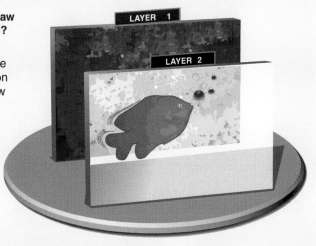

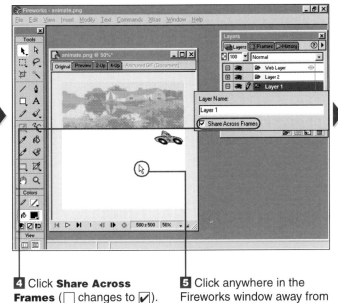

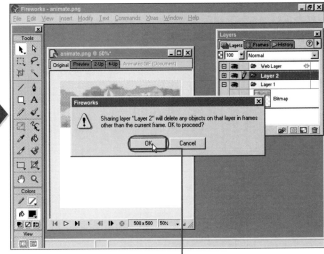

4 Click **Share Across
Frames** (☐ changes to ☑).

5 Click anywhere in the
Fireworks window away from
the Layer Name dialog box.

■ A warning dialog box
appears telling you that
Fireworks will delete any
objects on the layer that
are not in the current frame.

6 Click **OK**.

■ The layer appears
in all frames.

EDIT MULTIPLE FRAMES

You can select any item in any frame to edit when you turn on the Multi-Frame Editing option.

By default, the Multi-Frame Editing option is turned on.

EDIT MULTIPLE FRAMES

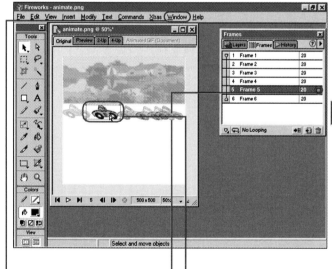

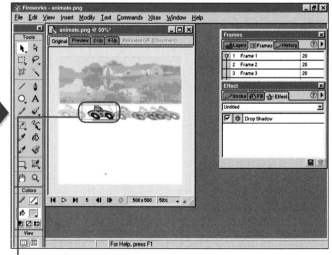

EDIT THE FRAMES

1 Click **Window** and then **Frames** to display the Frames panel.

2 Click the object in any frame to select it.

■ The blue selection icon (■) indicates the frame in which the selected item resides.

3 Edit the graphic.

Note: To move, transform, delete, or otherwise edit the graphic, see Chapter 4.

Why would I turn off Multi-Frame Editing?

You may want to turn off Multi-Frame Editing to select objects in the current frame only. Sometimes the ability to select objects in other frames gets in the way of editing the current frame.

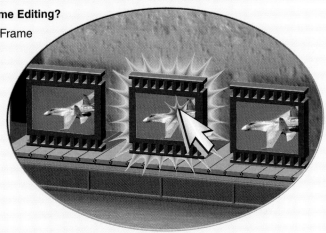

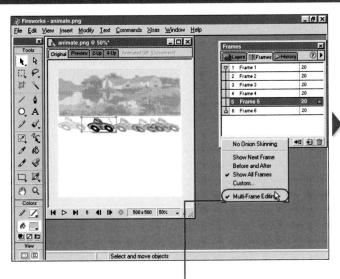

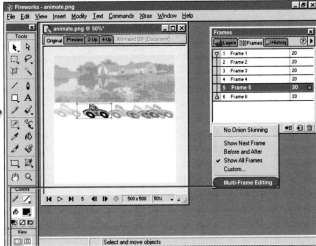

**TURN OFF
MULTI-FRAME EDITING**

1 Click 🖼️.

2 Click **Multi-Frame Editing**.

■ The check mark in front of the command disappears, indicating that the Multi-Frame Editing option is off.

■ You can repeat Steps **1** and **2** to turn on the Multi-Frame Editing option again.

SET ANIMATION REPEATS

Looping is the process of an animation repeating itself. You can set the animation to loop a specific number of times or over and over again.

SET ANIMATION REPEATS

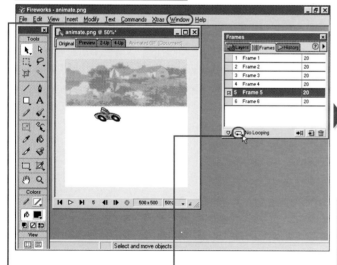

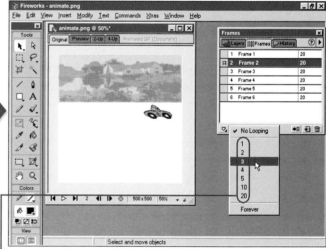

1 Click **Window** and then **Frames** to display the Frames panel.

2 Click the GIF Animation Looping button (▦).

■ A pop-up menu appears.

3 Click the number of times to loop the animation.

Note: The default is Forever.

■ The animation loops the number of times you specify.

You can preview an animation as you work to make sure that it is progressing the way you want.

PREVIEW AN ANIMATION

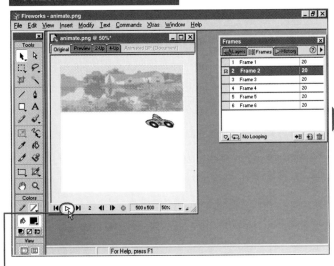 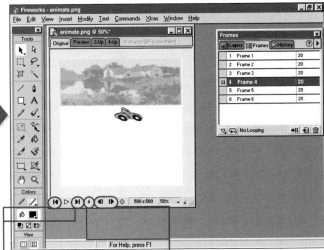

1 Click the Play button (▷).

■ ▷ changes to the Stop button (■).

■ The animation plays and continues to play until you click ■.

■ You can click the First Frame (◀◀) or Last Frame (▶▶) button to view the first or last frame, respectively.

■ You can click the Previous Frame (◀◀) or Next Frame (▶▶) button to view the previous or next frame, respectively.

■ This shows the number of the current frame.

CREATE INSTANCES

You can create *instances* of symbols in Fireworks to use as a basis for an animation. A *symbol* is the original from which you copy all instances. You can change instances without changing the original symbol.

For more information about symbols and instances, see Chapter 7.

CREATE INSTANCES

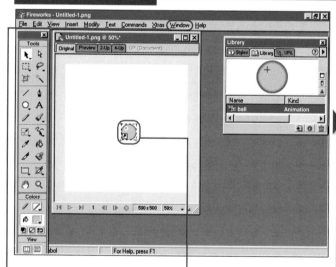

1 Click **Window** and then **Library** to open the Library panel.

2 Create or import a symbol.

Note: To find out about creating and importing a symbol, see Chapter 7.

■ You can delete the original symbol from the document by selecting the symbol and pressing `Delete`.

3 Click and drag the symbol in the library to the document.

4 Repeat Step **3** so that there are two instances in the document.

Why should I use instances in an animation instead of symbols?

Instances are simplified copies of the symbol. The symbol is a complex path object with fills and strokes. An instance is just a simple bitmap image that loads more quickly and improves animation performance.

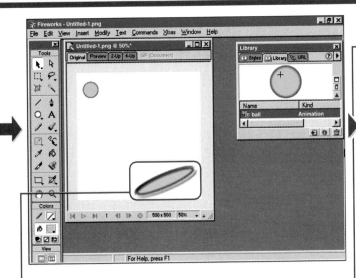

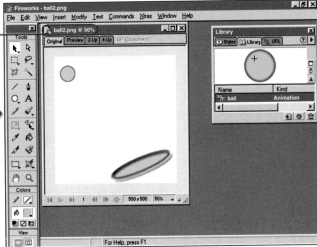

5 Make changes to one instance.

■ You can add text, add effects, or transform the second instance.

Note: For more information about changing an object, see Chapter 4.

6 Save the document.

Note: For more information about saving a document, see Chapter 2.

■ You can create multiple instances of the symbol.

■ You have a document ready to tween.

Note: For information about tweening, see the following section, "Tween Instances."

TWEEN INSTANCES

You can tween instances to create an animation. *Tweening* makes one object change into another similar object during the animation.

TWEEN INSTANCES

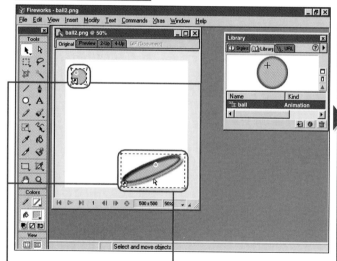

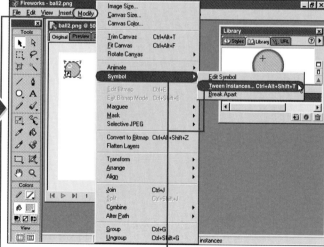

CREATE INSTANCES

1 Create instances.

Note: To create an instance, see the section "Create Instances."

2 Make changes to each instance.

■ You can make changes to the instances by adding effects or transforming the object.

3 Select two or more instances.

TWEEN THE INSTANCES

4 Click **Modify**.

5 Click **Symbol**.

6 Click **Tween Instances**.

What is tweening?

Tweening creates interim instances between two or more instances you draw. When you tween objects, Fireworks guesses what the in-between, or "tween," objects should look like and calculates their physical appearance. You can specify how

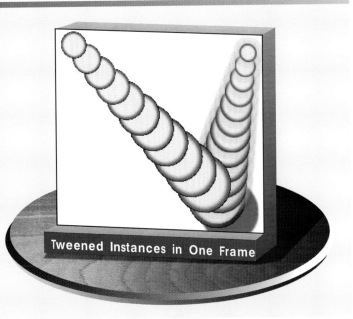

Tweened Instances in One Frame

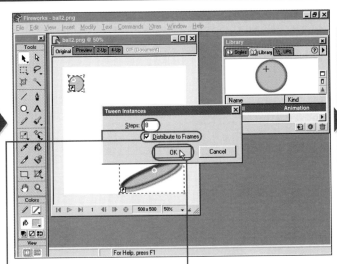

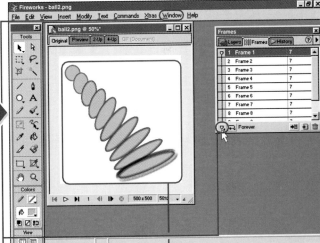

■ The Tween Instances dialog box appears.

7 Type the number of in-between instances you want in your animation in the Steps box.

8 Click **Distribute to Frames** (☐ changes to ✔).

9 Click **OK**.

■ All but the first symbol disappear. Fireworks calculates the frames in between the first and last instance and inserts each into a frame.

VIEW TWEENED FRAMES

10 Click **Window** and then **Frames** to display the Frames panel.

11 Click 🔲 and then **Show All Frames**.

■ You can see the frames used in the tweening.

Note: To play your animation, see the section "Preview an Animation."

237

SET FRAME DELAY

You can control how long each frame displays in the browser so that you can show some frames longer than others.

SET FRAME DELAY

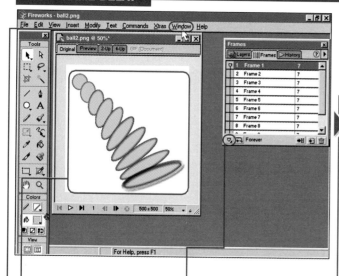

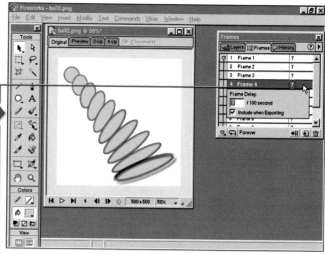

1 Create the animation.

2 Click **Window** and then **Frames** to display the Frames panel.

■ You can click [▦] and then **Show All Frames** to see all frames of the animation.

3 Double-click the number to the right of the frame that you want to delay.

■ To change the frame delay for multiple frames from one pop-up box, you can press **Shift** and click the number boxes.

■ A pop-up edit window appears.

How long does Fireworks show a frame?

The default frame delay is 20, which equals 20 hundredths of a second. 100 equals one second, 50 equals half a second, 25 equals a quarter second, and so on. You can enter a number higher than 100 if you want the frame to display longer than one second. The amount of time you delay a frame depends on the contents of the frame.

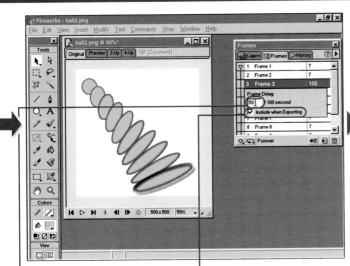

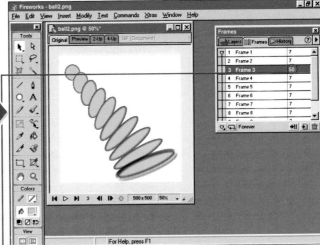

4 Type the delay you want for that one frame.

5 Click anywhere outside of the pop-up edit window.

■ Make sure that **Include When Exporting** is checked (☑) to ensure that the animation works correctly on a Web page.

■ The number you type in Step **4** appears in the Frames panel.

Note: To play your animation, see the section "Preview an Animation."

OPTIMIZE AN ANIMATION

You can optimize an animation so that the file is compressed for easier loading and exporting.

OPTIMIZE AN ANIMATION

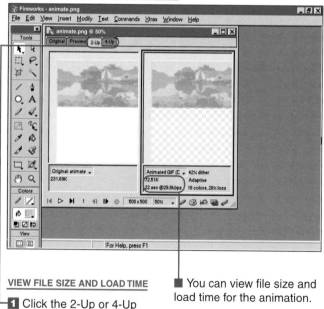

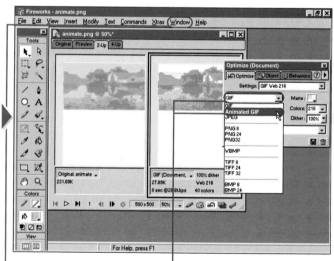

VIEW FILE SIZE AND LOAD TIME

1 Click the 2-Up or 4-Up preview tab.

■ You can view file size and load time for the animation.

SELECT AN EXPORT FILE FORMAT

2 Click **Window** and then **Optimize** to display the Optimize panel.

3 Click the Export File Format ▾.

4 Click **Animated GIF**.

Which color palette is best for animated GIF?

You can use any of the palettes for GIF; however, using Web 216 means that the colors are limited to Web-safe colors, which preserves your colors on most browsers. Try different palettes to see which looks the best with your animation.

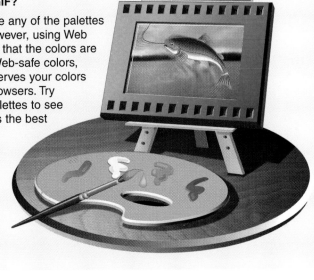

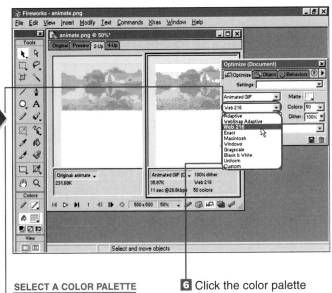

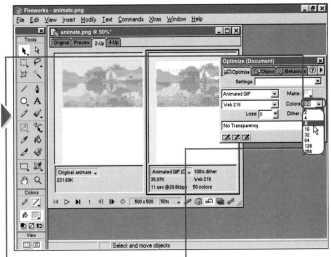

SELECT A COLOR PALETTE

5 Click the Indexed Palette ▾.

6 Click the color palette that you want to use.

■ You can compare the look of the animation in the two or four preview panes.

SELECT THE NUMBER OF COLORS

7 Click the Colors ▾.

8 Click the number of colors that you want Fireworks to use in your animation.

Note: Choose fewer colors to make the GIF file smaller.

CONTINUED

OPTIMIZE AN ANIMATION

You can choose settings for optimization that make the animated file smaller without losing colors and effects.

OPTIMIZE AN ANIMATION (CONTINUED)

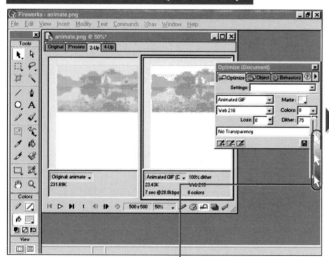

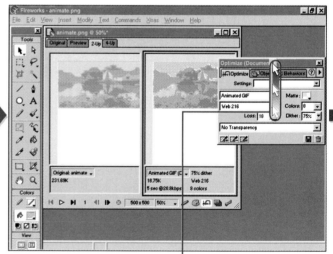

ADJUST DITHER

Note: Dithering makes an animation look like it has more colors without increasing file size much.

9 Click the Dither ▾.

10 Adjust the slider to select the amount of dithering you want in your animation.

Note: Start with 50% dithering to see how the picture looks. Adjust the dithering from there to make the picture look the way you want.

ADJUST LOSS

Note: Loss lowers file size by deleting some detail. The image does distort some.

11 Click the Loss ▾.

12 Adjust the slider to the amount of loss that you want.

Note: Adjust loss a small amount and see how it affects the picture before you decide on another adjustment.

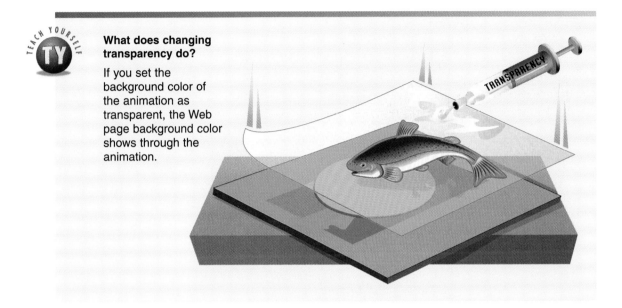

What does changing transparency do?

If you set the background color of the animation as transparent, the Web page background color shows through the animation.

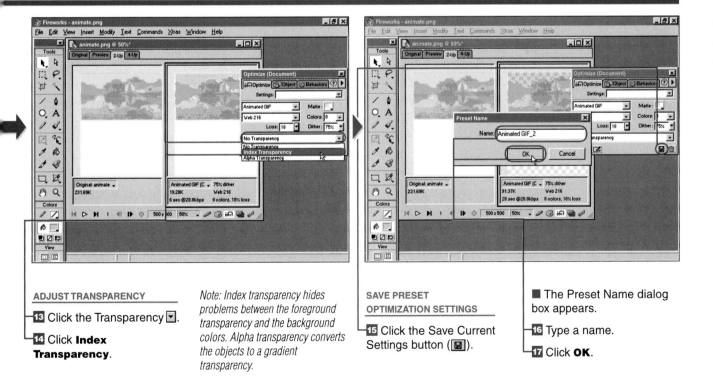

ADJUST TRANSPARENCY

13 Click the Transparency ▾.

14 Click **Index Transparency**.

Note: Index transparency hides problems between the foreground transparency and the background colors. Alpha transparency converts the objects to a gradient transparency.

SAVE PRESET OPTIMIZATION SETTINGS

15 Click the Save Current Settings button (🖫).

■ The Preset Name dialog box appears.

16 Type a name.

17 Click **OK**.

OPEN EXISTING ANIMATIONS

You can open any vector drawing from FreeHand, Illustrator, or CorelDRAW and then make changes to it in Fireworks.

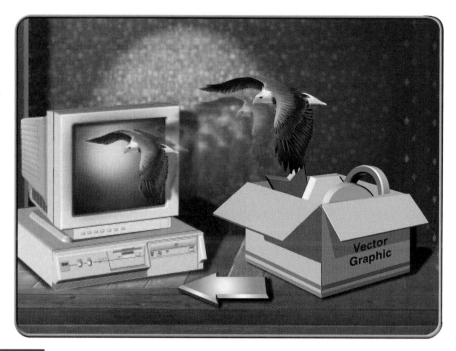

OPEN EXISTING ANIMATIONS

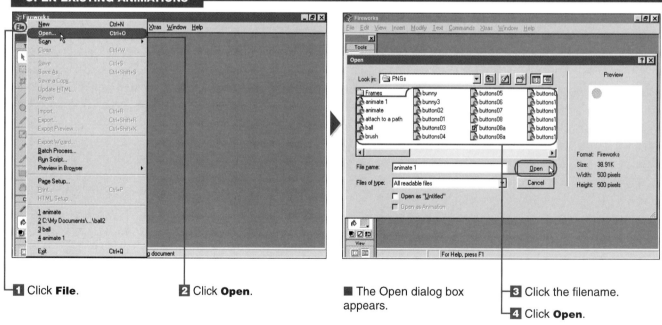

■1 Click **File**.

■2 Click **Open**.

■ The Open dialog box appears.

■3 Click the filename.

■4 Click **Open**.

My drawing does not look the same in Fireworks as it did in CorelDRAW. Why not?

Because Fireworks and CorelDRAW support different features, some changes occur when you open a CorelDRAW file in Fireworks. You may see changes in colors, grouped objects, dimensions, and text formatting.

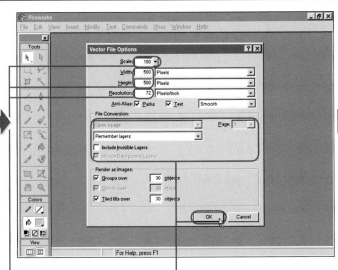

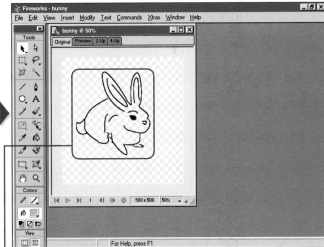

■ The Vector File Options dialog box appears.

5 Click the Scale ▼ and set the scale.

6 Type the width and height.

7 Type the resolution.

Note: Scale sets the size of the image against the original size; width and height set the actual size of the animation; and resolution defines the quality of the animation.

8 Type any other options for file conversion.

9 Click **OK**.

■ The image appears in the document area, and Fireworks translates the document to PNG format.

■ You can make any changes that you want to the animation and save it.

Note: See Chapter 2 for more on saving.

CHAPTER 12

Optimize Graphics

Do you want to compress your graphics to make them load quickly? This chapter shows you how to optimize graphics.

SELECT A GRAPHIC FILE FORMAT

You can use the file format that best suits the graphic so that the file loads quickly and looks its best.

FILE COMPRESSION

You want to use a file format that allows for compression so that file transfer over the Internet is fast.

GRAPHIC QUALITY

You lose some of your graphics' quality when you compress them. The different file formats have varying levels of quality because they use different types of compression. You can use the Fireworks Preview to check various formats.

PNG

Portable Network Graphic (PNG) is a flexible Web graphic format; some Web browsers, however, cannot view PNG. PNG is the original Fireworks file format. You can use PNG for line art and for images.

JPEG

The Joint Photographic Experts Group (JPEG) format is perfect for photographs, scanned images, images with textures, and gradient color objects.

GIF

The Graphics Interchange File (GIF) format is used for static or animated graphics. Use the GIF format for logos, cartoons, animations, and vector objects.

DESIGN FOR OPTIMIZATION

You can design graphics so that they are easier to optimize when you are ready to export the graphics.

CROP GRAPHICS

Crop all graphics and images so that they are as small as they can be (see Chapter 5). After you crop your graphics, you can click **Modify** and then click **Trim Canvas** to make your graphics even smaller.

COLORS

Limit the number of colors, if possible, in any graphic or text. Choose the appropriate palette for the file type. Fireworks includes palettes specifically designed for Windows and for the Macintosh, for example.

COLOR AND GIFS

When designing a GIF graphic, use solid colors or horizontal stripes of color. Stripes and large areas of color compress well within the GIF format.

COLOR AND JPEGS

Use the JPEG format when an image or graphic uses more than 256 colors. You can adjust the quality to make up for using lots of colors.

GAMMA MODE

Macintosh Gamma mode in Windows and Windows Gamma mode on the Macintosh modify the display to show you how your graphic would look on another computer. Gamma mode is under the View menu.

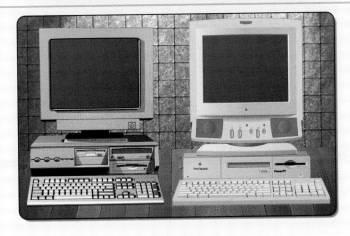

OPTIMIZE WITH THE COLOR TABLE

You can use the Color Table panel to limit the file size of your color images and graphics. Limiting the number of colors limits the file size.

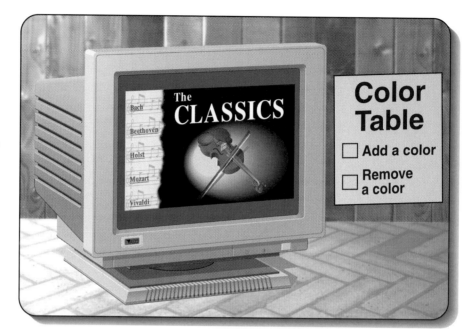

REBUILD THE COLOR TABLE

Note: If the word Rebuild *displays in the Color Table title bar, the colors in the Color Table are out of date.*

1 Display the graphic.

2 Click **Window** and then **Color Table** to display the Color Table.

3 Click the Options.

4 Click **Rebuild Color Table**.

■ You can see the number of colors used in the graphic in the Color Table panel.

What do the different types of icons in the Color Table mean?

The icons represent different types of colors and actions that you have taken to those colors. For example, they can tell you if the color is Web-safe, if you have shifted to a Web-safe color, or if the color is locked.

Selected Color

Web–Safe Color

Shifted to a Web–Safe Color

Locked Color

LOCATE COLORS AND MAKE THEM WEB-SAFE

LOCATE A GRAPHIC'S COLOR IN THE COLOR TABLE

■1 Move ⌐ over the graphic.

■ The color under ⌐ becomes highlighted.

MAKE A COLOR WEB-SAFE

■1 Click any color in the Color Table.

■2 Click the Snap to Web Safe button (🔲).

Note: Web-safe colors are colors common to both the Macintosh and Windows platforms and so display well in any browser.

CONTINUED

OPTIMIZE WITH THE COLOR TABLE

You can choose the colors you want to keep before you reduce the number of colors in a graphic.

LOCK COLORS

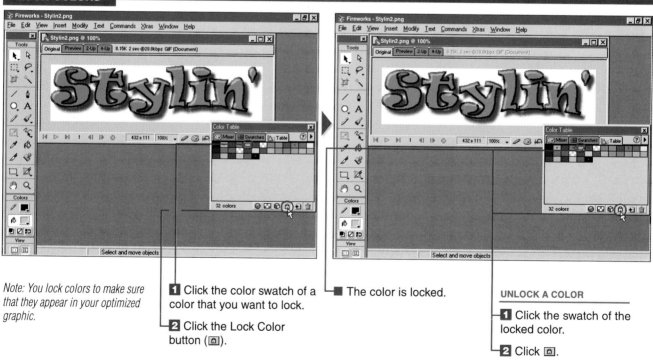

Note: You lock colors to make sure that they appear in your optimized graphic.

1 Click the color swatch of a color that you want to lock.

2 Click the Lock Color button (🔒).

■ The color is locked.

UNLOCK A COLOR

1 Click the swatch of the locked color.

2 Click 🔒.

254

What happens if I lock some colors and then change palettes or reduce the number of colors in my graphic?

The locked colors appear in the new palette if you change palettes. Locked colors remain in the reduced number of colors as well.

ADD OR DELETE COLORS

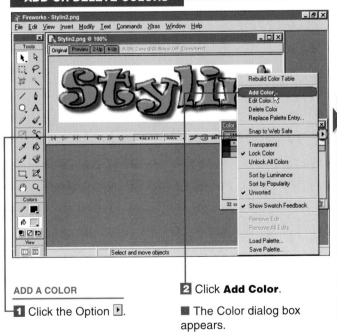

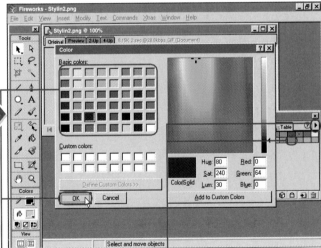

ADD A COLOR

1 Click the Option ▶.

2 Click **Add Color**.

■ The Color dialog box appears.

3 Click the color that you want to add.

4 Click **OK**.

■ The color appears in the Color Table.

DELETE A COLOR

1 Click the color's swatch.

2 Click the Option ▶.

3 Click **Delete Color**.

■ The color is deleted from the Color Table.

OPTIMIZE PNGS AND GIFS

You can optimize
PNG and GIF
graphics before
you export them to
make sure that
they load on to the
Web page quickly.

You use similar
optimization settings
for PNGs and GIFs.

OPTIMIZE PNGS AND GIFS

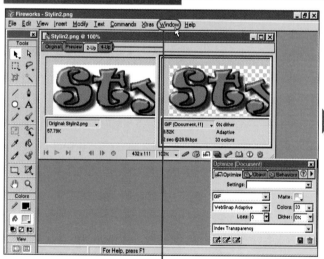

CHOOSE THE FILE FORMAT

*Note: You can use the different views
to compare optimization settings.
The different windows also show
how fast the graphic downloads in
different formats.*

1 Open the graphic in
Preview, 2-Up, or 4-Up view.

2 Click **Window** and then
Optimize to display the
Optimize panel.

3 Click the Export File
Format ▼.

4 Click the file format that
you want to use.

*Note: Between PNG and GIF, GIF is
the better file format to use for Web
graphics.*

■ The graphic changes to
the file format that you
specified.

How does changing the indexed palette affect the changes I make in the Color Table?

The colors remain similar. The difference is whether the colors are suitable for the Web. WebSnap Adaptive or Web 216 are best for Internet graphics.

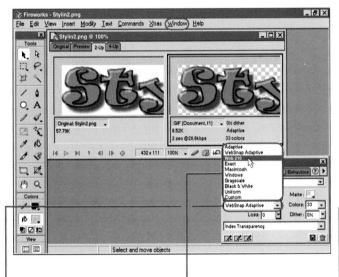

CHOOSE A COLOR PALETTE

1 Click the Indexed Palette ▾.

2 Click the color palette that you want to use.

Note: For more information about color palettes, see Chapter 11.

■ The color palette changes to the one that you selected.

CHOOSE THE NUMBER OF COLORS

1 Click the Maximum Number of Colors ▾.

2 Click the number of colors.

Note: The fewer colors you use, the smaller the graphic file will be.

■ The number of colors changes to what you specified.

CONTINUED ▶

OPTIMIZE PNGS AND GIFS

You can make the canvas color and other colors appear transparent so that the Web page's background color shows through a portion of the graphic.

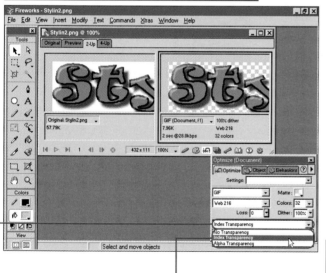

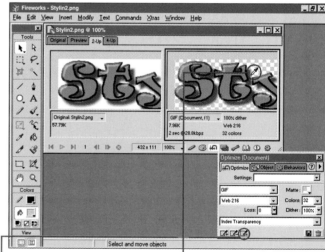

SET A TRANSPARENT BACKGROUND

1 Click the Choose Type of Transparency 🔽.

2 Click the type of transparency that you want.

■ Transparent colors appear as a checkerboard pattern.

SET A TRANSPARENT COLOR

1 Click the Set Transparent Index Color button (🖾) (🔱 changes to 🖋).

2 Click the color in the graphic that you want to be transparent.

■ Every instance of that color in the graphic becomes transparent.

258

What is the difference between index and alpha transparency?

Index transparency makes the selected color or canvas transparent. If you choose to make white transparent, for example, index transparency makes everything white in the graphic, plus the canvas, transparent. Alpha transparency makes a color appear transparent when viewed in a Web browser. You can use alpha transparency to touch up the color around a graphic so that it does not bleed into the background of the Web page.

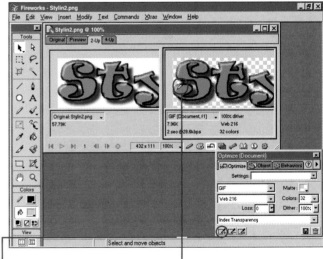

DESELECT TRANSPARENT COLORS

1 Click the Remove Color from Transparency button (🖾) to deselect a color.

2 Click the transparent color in the graphic.

■ The transparent color changes back to its original color.

SELECT A TRANSPARENT COLOR

1 Click the Add Color to Transparency button (🖾).

2 Click the color in the graphic.

■ The selected color becomes transparent.

OPTIMIZE JPEGS

You can optimize a JPEG to create a smaller file and speed loading time.

Optimizing a JPEG reduces the quality of the image.

OPTIMIZE JPEGS

1 Open the Preview, 2-Up, or 4-Up view of the image.

2 Click **Window** and then **Optimize** to display the Optimize panel.

■ If the file format is not already JPEG, you can click ▼ to change it to JPEG.

3 Click the Quality ▼.

4 Click and drag the slider to indicate the quality.

How do I decide which quality setting to use?

Quality is measured in percentage — from 0 to 100 percent. The higher the percentage, the more quality yet less compression in the graphic. You can lower the quality percentage quite a bit before you notice changes in the image.

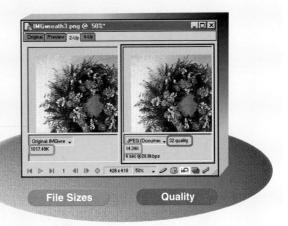

File Sizes   Quality

5 Click the Smoothing Level ⏷.

6 Click the number that you want to use.

Note: Smoothing blurs the entire image so that the results of the compression are less noticeable. You can start with a 4 or 5 and see how the picture looks before you change it to a higher or lower number.

7 Click the Options ▶.

8 Confirm that **Remove Unused Colors** is checked.

Note: Clicking the command when it is checked removes the check mark.

■ The JPEG is optimized for export.

OPTIMIZE A SLICE

You can optimize slices of the whole graphic so that images export as JPEG and text exports as a GIF, for example.

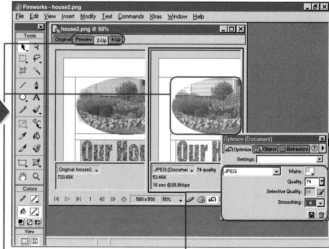

1 Display the document.

2 Click **Window** and then **Optimize** to display the Optimize panel.

3 Choose the Preview, 2-Up, or 4-Up view.

4 Select the slice that you want to optimize.

5 Optimize the slice by choosing the file format, palette, number of colors, and dithering for GIFs, or quality and smoothing for JPEGs.

■ You can select another slice for optimization as well.

You can save
optimization settings so
that you can apply them
to other graphics and
images.

SAVE OPTIMIZATION SETTINGS

1 Optimize a graphic or
image.

■ You can save the same
optimization settings to use
for other similar graphics or
images.

2 Click the Options ▶.

3 Click **Save Settings**.

■ The Preset Name dialog
box appears.

4 Type the name of the
setting.

5 Click **OK**.

APPLY SAVED SETTINGS

1 Click the Options ▶.

2 Click the name of the
saved setting.

IMAGE MAP
HTML file
BUTTONS
FOR EXPORT
IMAGE MAPS
FOR EXPORT

CHAPTER 13

Export Objects and Slices

Are you ready to export your graphics to other programs, such as FrontPage or Dreamweaver? This chapter shows you how to set the options and export objects and slices.

You can look at your document in Export Preview to check optimization settings before you export the graphic.

OPEN EXPORT PREVIEW

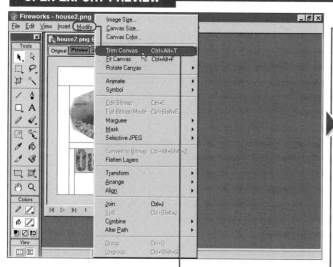

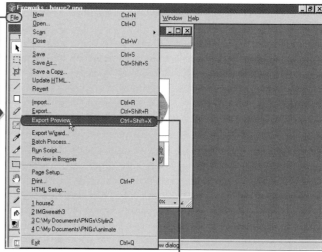

1 Open the document.

Note: Before exporting, it is a good idea to trim your graphic to remove unnecessary canvas.

■ To do so, you can click **Modify** and then **Trim Canvas**.

2 Click **File**.

3 Click **Export Preview**.

■ The Export Preview dialog box appears.

You can use the optimization and other options to prepare the graphic or image for exporting to another program.

Number of Colors

Color Table Options Pop-up Menu Button

Tabbed Panels

File Information

File Format

Color Palette

Optimization Settings

Color Table

Color Table Buttons

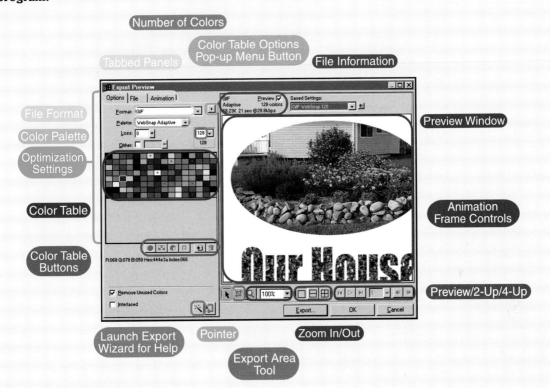

Preview Window

Animation Frame Controls

Preview/2-Up/4-Up

Launch Export Wizard for Help

Pointer

Zoom In/Out

Export Area Tool

EXPORT AN AREA OR AN ENTIRE GRAPHIC OR IMAGE

You can select any area of the Fireworks document to export only that area.

EXPORT AN AREA

Note: To export an entire graphic or image, skip to the subsection "Export an Entire Graphic or Image."

■ **1** Open the Export Preview window (see the section "Open Export Preview").

■ You can check optimization settings and make changes to those settings now.

■ **2** Click ☑ and zoom out to see the entire area to be exported.

■ **3** Click the Export Area tool (⬚).

■ A rectangular border and eight handles appear around the graphic.

Can I optimize my graphic in the Export Preview window instead of using the Optimize panel?

Yes. If you prefer, you can open a graphic or image in the Export Preview window and perform all optimization adjustments just before you export the graphic.

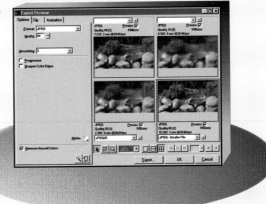

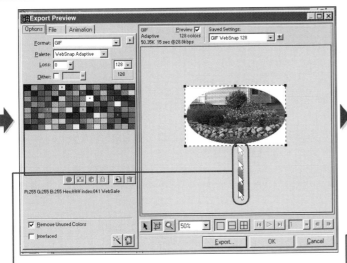

4 Click and drag the handles to define the area that you want to export.

5 Click the Pointer tool (▶).

Note: Click the graphic that you want to export, if you have 2-Up or 4-Up view open.

6 Click **Export**.

■ The Export dialog box appears.

7 Skip to Step **3** of the subsection "Export an Entire Graphic or Image."

CONTINUED

EXPORT AN AREA OR AN ENTIRE GRAPHIC OR IMAGE

You can choose to export a graphic or image from the Export Preview dialog box or from the File menu.

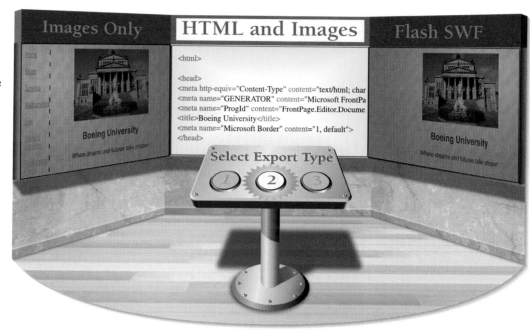

EXPORT AN ENTIRE GRAPHIC OR IMAGE

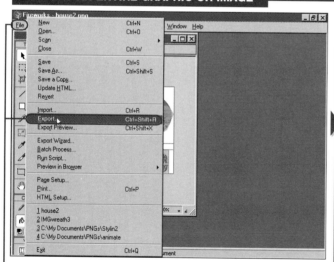

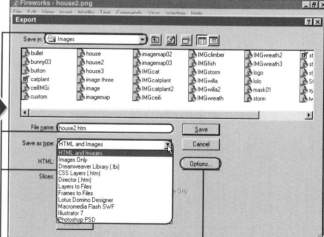

1 Click **File**.

2 Click **Export**.

*Note: From the Export Preview window, you can click **Export** to open the Export dialog box.*

■ The Export dialog box appears.

3 Click ⬇ and choose a folder.

4 Type a name or accept the name that Fireworks provides.

5 Click the Save as Type ⬇ and select a file type.

*Note: To export only an image, click **Images Only**.*

■ If you choose **HTML and Images**, click **Options**.

*Note: If you do not choose **HTML and Images**, skip to Step **6**.*

Which file type should I save the file as?

If you export the file to another program — such as Illustrator, Flash, or Photoshop — to continue work on the file, choose that file type. If you export the file for use in another program — such as Dreamweaver or FrontPage, you can save the file as HTML and Images.

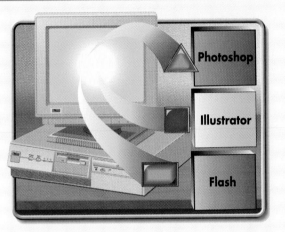

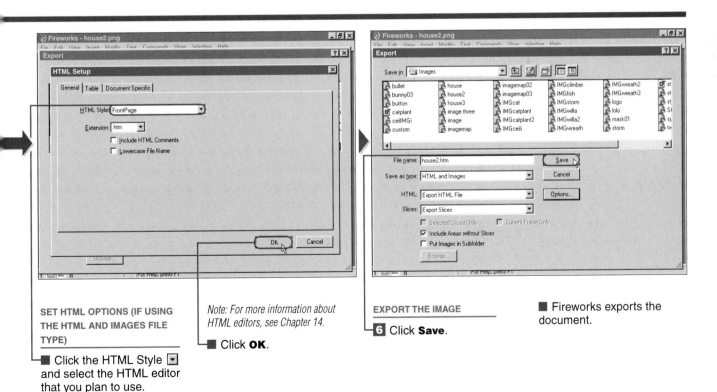

SET HTML OPTIONS (IF USING THE HTML AND IMAGES FILE TYPE)

■ Click the HTML Style ▾ and select the HTML editor that you plan to use.

Note: For more information about HTML editors, see Chapter 14.

■ Click **OK**.

EXPORT THE IMAGE

6 Click **Save**.

■ Fireworks exports the document.

EXPORT A SLICE

You can export one slice
from any graphic to save
load time and limit file
size.

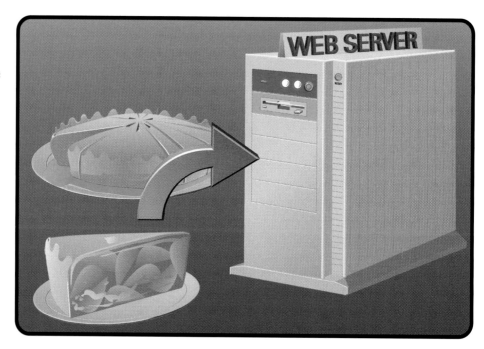

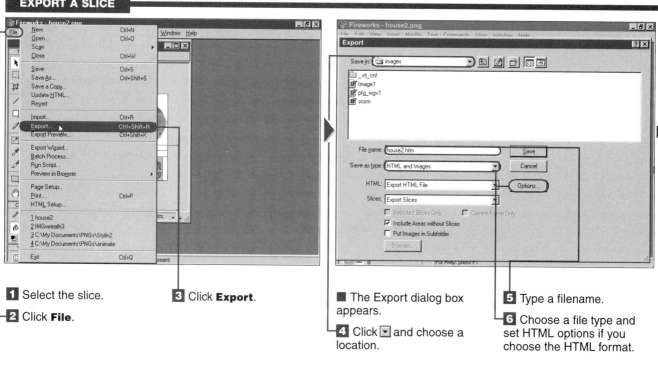

1 Select the slice.

2 Click **File**.

3 Click **Export**.

■ The Export dialog box
appears.

4 Click ▼ and choose a
location.

5 Type a filename.

6 Choose a file type and
set HTML options if you
choose the HTML format.

Should I choose Export Slices or Slice Along Guides in the Export dialog box?

Generally, choose **Export Slices**. Choose **Slice Along Guides** to divide a large image into multiple slices using the guides and only when there are no behaviors attached to the image.

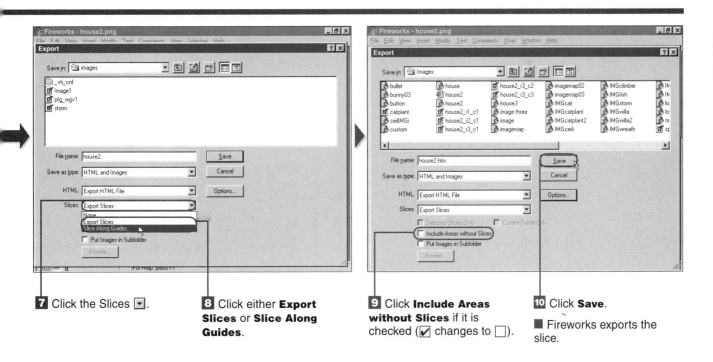

7 Click the Slices ▼.

8 Click either **Export Slices** or **Slice Along Guides**.

9 Click **Include Areas without Slices** if it is checked (☑ changes to ☐).

10 Click **Save**.

■ Fireworks exports the slice.

EXPORT LAYERS OR FRAMES

You can export layers or frames as separate image files so that each layer or frame file is smaller than the original file.

EXPORT LAYERS OR FRAMES

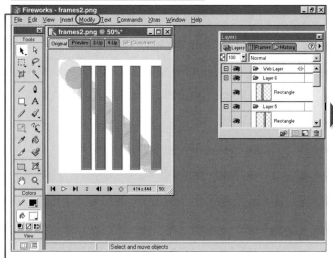

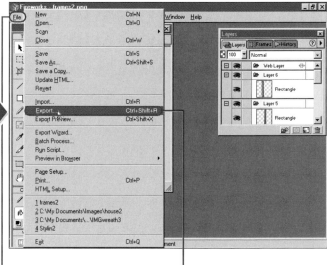

Note: Before exporting, you should optimize your graphic (see Chapter 12) and trim its canvas.

■ To trim the canvas, you can click **Modify** and then **Trim Canvas**.

■ The canvas trims to include all graphics in all frames or layers.

■1 Click **File**.

■2 Click **Export**.

How does Fireworks name files when you export a graphic or image?

When you export layers or frames, Fireworks names each file with the document name and the name of the layer or frame. For example, a frame filename might be house_f13; house is the name of the document, and _f13 is the frame. You can change the name of the document when you type the filename in the Export dialog box.

DOCName_f03

DOCName_f02

DOCName_f01

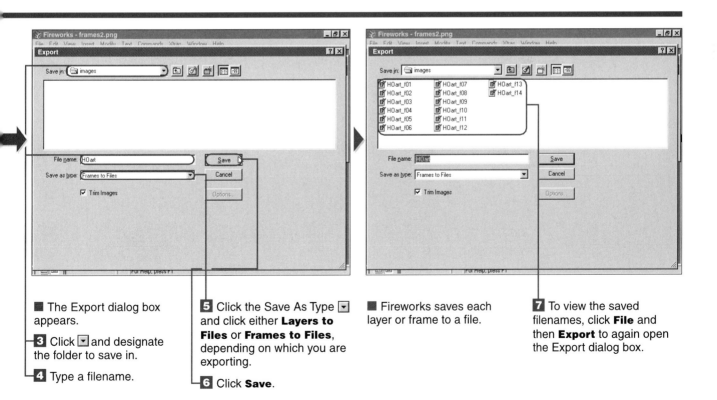

■ The Export dialog box appears.

3 Click ▼ and designate the folder to save in.

4 Type a filename.

5 Click the Save As Type ▼ and click either **Layers to Files** or **Frames to Files**, depending on which you are exporting.

6 Click **Save**.

■ Fireworks saves each layer or frame to a file.

7 To view the saved filenames, click **File** and then **Export** to again open the Export dialog box.

EXPORT AN ANIMATION

You can export an
animation to another
program to work on it
or to display it on your
Web page.

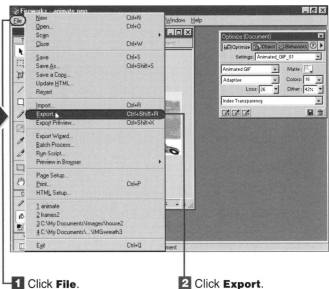

Note: Before exporting, it is a good idea to optimize your graphic (see Chapter 12).

■ To do so, use the Optimize panel (click **Window** and then **Optimize**).

■1 Click **File**.

■2 Click **Export**.

To which file types can I export an animation?

You can export an animation to Flash SWF format or Photoshop PSD format, for example, to work on the animation graphic further. Export to Animated GIF to display the animation in an HTML editor, such as Dreamweaver.

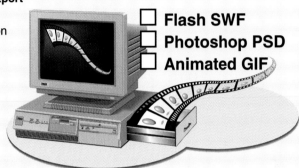

☐ **Flash SWF**
☐ **Photoshop PSD**
☐ **Animated GIF**

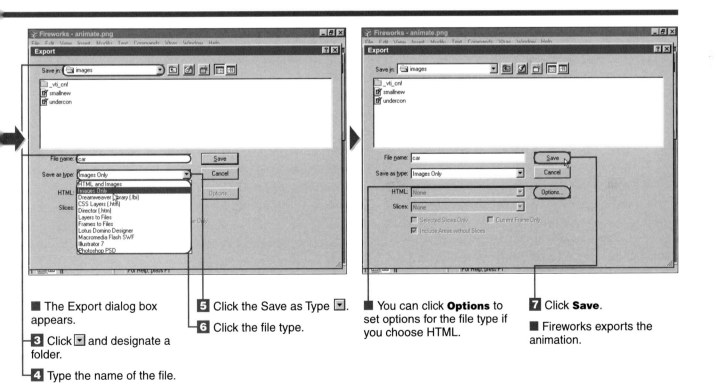

■ The Export dialog box appears.

3 Click ⏷ and designate a folder.

4 Type the name of the file.

5 Click the Save as Type ⏷.

6 Click the file type.

■ You can click **Options** to set options for the file type if you choose HTML.

7 Click **Save**.

■ Fireworks exports the animation.

EXPORT AN IMAGE MAP

You can export an image map to an HTML file format. Until you export the image map, it does not function as an image map in the Web browser.

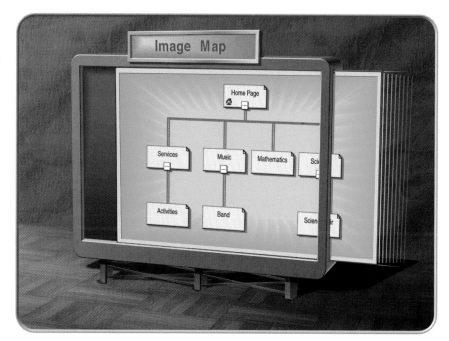

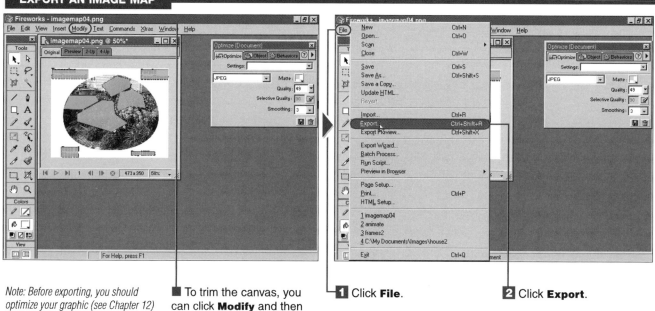

Note: Before exporting, you should optimize your graphic (see Chapter 12) and trim its canvas.

■ To trim the canvas, you can click **Modify** and then **Trim Canvas**.

1 Click **File**.

2 Click **Export**.

**What does the exported
image map file contain?**

The exported image
map file contains
the graphic file, the
HTML file, and all
the information for
hotspots and
URL links.

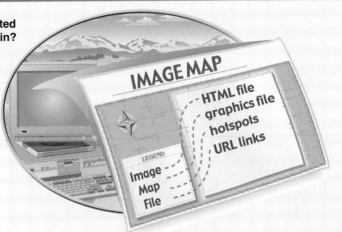

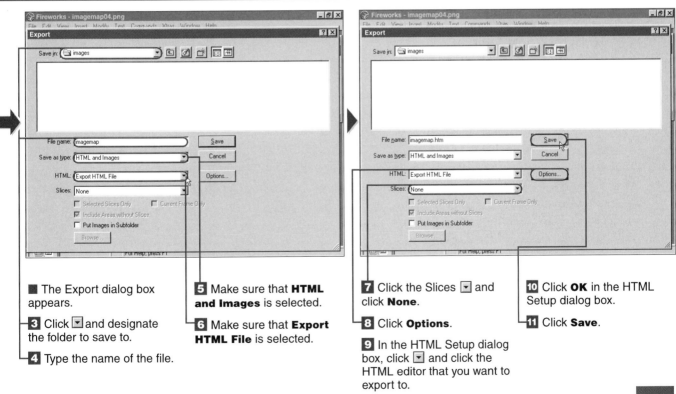

■ The Export dialog box
appears.

3 Click ▼ and designate
the folder to save to.

4 Type the name of the file.

5 Make sure that **HTML
and Images** is selected.

6 Make sure that **Export
HTML File** is selected.

7 Click the Slices ▼ and
click **None**.

8 Click **Options**.

9 In the HTML Setup dialog
box, click ▼ and click the
HTML editor that you want to
export to.

10 Click **OK** in the HTML
Setup dialog box.

11 Click **Save**.

CHAPTER 14

Integrate Fireworks Graphics with HTML Editors

Would you like to use your Fireworks graphics on your Web page? This chapter shows you how to use Fireworks with HTML editors.

HTML OVERVIEW

Although Fireworks generates the HTML codes for your Fireworks graphics, you can work with HTML by inserting code into your HTML editor.

HTML FILES

Hypertext Markup Language (HTML) files contain text and tags. Tags define the text, page format, and page structure. Fireworks creates the HTML file. You can copy the file into other programs.

HTML EDITORS

An HTML editor is a program in which you create Web pages (see the section "HTML Editors Overview"). You can use various HTML editors with your Fireworks graphics, including Dreamweaver, FrontPage, and GoLive.

HTML AND EXPORTING

When you export Fireworks graphics, you set HTML properties to ensure that you can use the graphic in the HTML editor. See Chapter 13 for information about exporting.

WEB BROWSERS

Web browsers, such as Internet Explorer and Netscape Navigator, translate HTML code into formatted Web pages. To view a Web page's HTML code in your browser, first display the Web page. Then click **View** and then **Source** in Internet Explorer or **View** and then **Page Source** in Netscape Navigator.

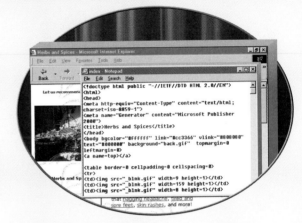

HTML TAGS

HTML tags are made up of text in angle brackets. Web browsers translate the tags to format the text in between the beginning and ending tags. For example, a Web browser formats any text between the tags <head> and </head> as a heading.

FIREWORKS AND HTML

You do not have to work directly with HTML in Fireworks because Fireworks automatically generates HTML for you. You may, however, work with HTML code when copying pieces of documents, for example.

HTML EDITORS OVERVIEW

You can use an HTML editor to create Web pages using Fireworks graphics and other text and image elements.

WHAT IS AN HTML EDITOR?

An HTML editor is a program in which you create Web pages. Most HTML editors automatically enter HTML tags using standard menus and dialog boxes. These HTML editors display the page on-screen, in a preview view.

WHAT CAN I DO WITH AN HTML EDITOR?

With an HTML editor, you can create and format text and other elements that go together to produce Web pages and Web sites.

HOW DOES FIREWORKS FIT IN WITH HTML EDITORS?

You can export Fireworks animations, buttons, rollovers, and other graphics to an HTML editor to help create professional-looking, interactive Web pages.

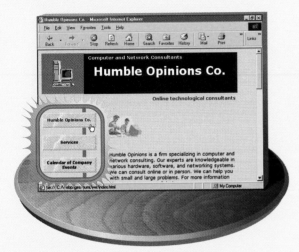

MICROSOFT FRONTPAGE

Microsoft FrontPage is a popular HTML editor. If you are used to Microsoft Office programs, FrontPage may be easier for you to learn to use than other HTML editors.

MACROMEDIA DREAMWEAVER

Macromedia Dreamweaver is another popular HTML editor. Because Dreamweaver and Fireworks are both made by Macromedia, you may prefer to use Dreamweaver as your HTML editor. Dreamweaver and Fireworks share many of the same features and toolbars, as well as many procedures, which makes the two work well together and may make Dreamweaver easy for you to learn.

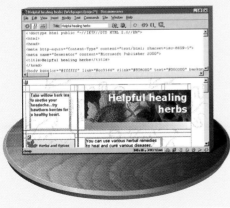

OTHER HTML EDITORS

You may use any of the numerous other HTML editors with Fireworks. Adobe GoLive and Optima PageSpinner are two other HTML editors you may want to try. GoLive is an easy program to learn; it is similar to a desktop publishing program. PageSpinner is a Web-authoring program for the Macintosh, and both beginning and advanced Web designers can use it.

COPY AND PASTE HTML

You can copy HTML code to the Clipboard and then paste the code into an HTML editor.

COPY AND PASTE HTML

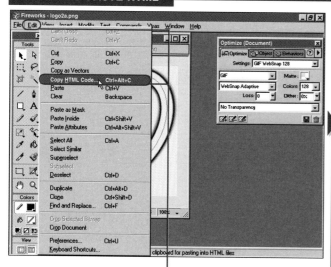

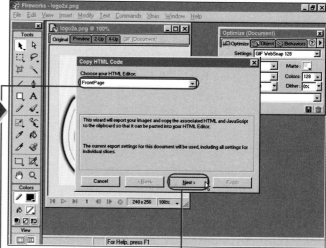

COPY HTML

Note: It is a good idea to optimize and prepare the graphic for exporting before copying and pasting the HTML (see Chapters 12 and 13).

1 Select the graphic to be copied.

2 Click **Edit**.

3 Click **Copy HTML Code**.

■ The Copy HTML Code dialog box appears.

4 Click the HTML Editor ▼ and select the editor that you plan to use.

5 Click **Next**.

Does it matter to which folder I save the HTML file?

If you use Dreamweaver, the HTML file saves automatically to the right folder. If you use a different HTML editor, you must save the Fireworks HTML file to the same folder as the HTML document in the HTML editor.

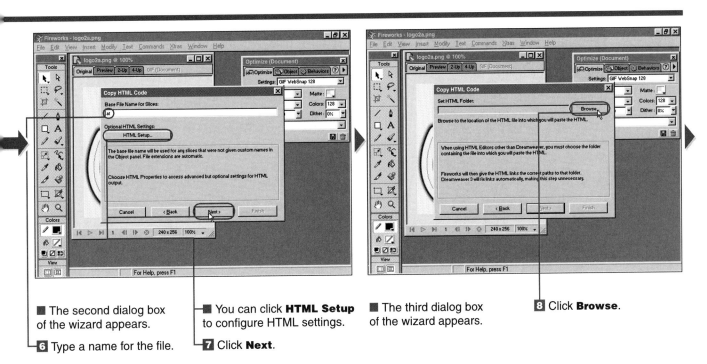

■ The second dialog box of the wizard appears.

6 Type a name for the file.

■ You can click **HTML Setup** to configure HTML settings.

7 Click **Next**.

■ The third dialog box of the wizard appears.

8 Click **Browse**.

CONTINUED

COPY AND PASTE HTML

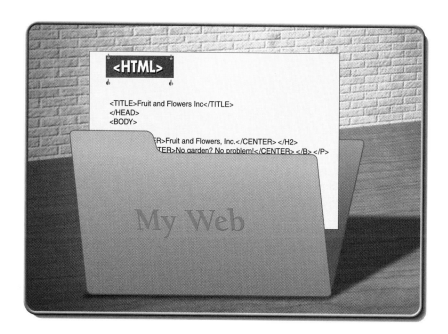

You can paste the HTML into a folder where all images are exported.

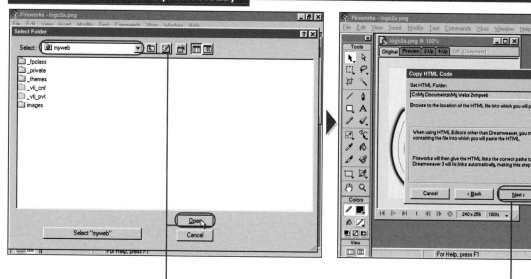

■ The Select Folder dialog box appears.

9 Click ▼ and choose the destination folder.

10 Click **Open**.

■ The Select Folder dialog box closes, returning you to the Copy HTML Code dialog box.

11 Click **Next**.

■ The next dialog box of the wizard appears, in which you choose a folder for saving your exported images.

**Why do I have to set up two
HTML folders?**

When you choose an HTML
editor other than Dreamweaver,
you must set up an extra HTML
folder to hold the file that you
are pasting. When you choose
Dreamweaver as your HTML
editor, Dreamweaver
automatically corrects paths
and links to the file.

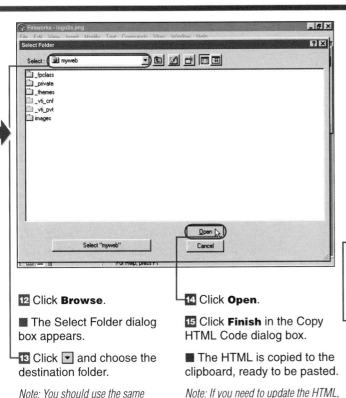

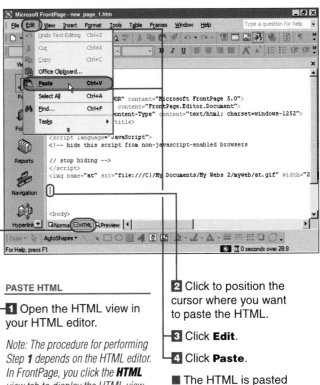

12 Click **Browse**.

■ The Select Folder dialog
box appears.

13 Click ▼ and choose the
destination folder.

*Note: You should use the same
folder used in Step 9.*

14 Click **Open**.

15 Click **Finish** in the Copy
HTML Code dialog box.

■ The HTML is copied to the
clipboard, ready to be pasted.

*Note: If you need to update the HTML,
you can export the HTML again and
overwrite the older file.*

PASTE HTML

1 Open the HTML view in
your HTML editor.

*Note: The procedure for performing
Step 1 depends on the HTML editor.
In FrontPage, you click the **HTML**
view tab to display the HTML view.*

2 Click to position the
cursor where you want
to paste the HTML.

3 Click **Edit**.

4 Click **Paste**.

■ The HTML is pasted
into the document.

COPY HTML FOR SLICED OBJECTS

You can copy HTML code for a sliced object or multiple objects in the Fireworks document.

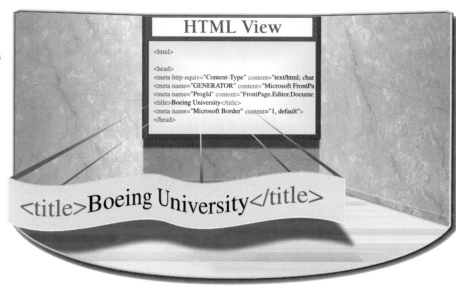

View the HTML code in a text editor and copy just the code you need.

COPY HTML FOR SLICED OBJECTS

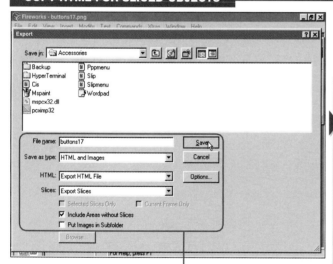 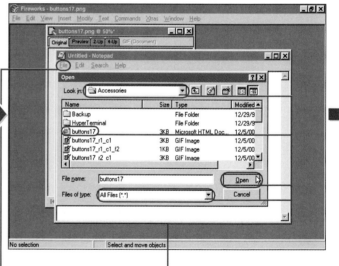

1 Select one or more slices in the Fireworks document.

2 Click **File** and then **Export**.

■ The Export dialog box appears.

3 Export the slices (see Chapter 13).

*Note: Select **HTML and Images** as the type. In the HTML Setup dialog box, select **Generic** as the HTML style.*

Note: Export the HTML file to the same folder as your HTML editor.

4 Open a text editor, such as Notepad.

5 Open the HTML document.

■ To do so in Notepad, first click **File** and then **Open**.

■ Click the Look In ▼ and browse to the folder where you exported the slice file.

■ Click the Files of Type ▼ and select **All Files**.

■ Click the name of the HTML document and then click **Open**.

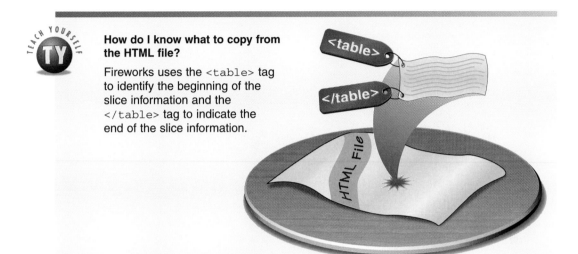

How do I know what to copy from the HTML file?

Fireworks uses the `<table>` tag to identify the beginning of the slice information and the `</table>` tag to indicate the end of the slice information.

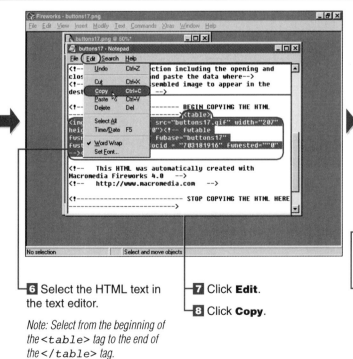

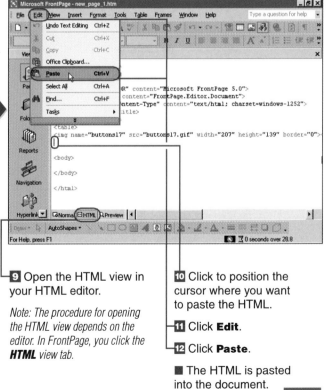

6 Select the HTML text in the text editor.

Note: Select from the beginning of the `<table>` tag to the end of the `</table>` tag.

7 Click **Edit**.

8 Click **Copy**.

9 Open the HTML view in your HTML editor.

*Note: The procedure for opening the HTML view depends on the editor. In FrontPage, you click the **HTML** view tab.*

10 Click to position the cursor where you want to paste the HTML.

11 Click **Edit**.

12 Click **Paste**.

■ The HTML is pasted into the document.

COPY JAVASCRIPT

You can copy buttons
and other JavaScript
from Fireworks
documents to your
HTML editor.

COPY JAVASCRIPT

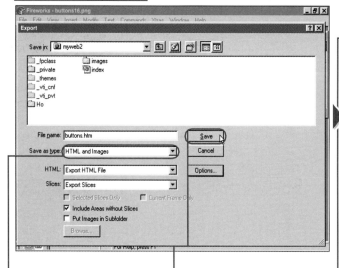

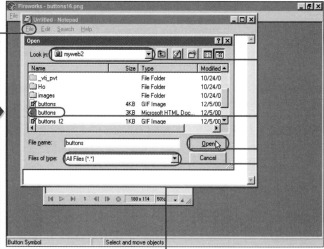

1 Open the sliced file in
Fireworks.

*Note: Optimize the graphic. For more
information, see Chapter 12.*

2 Click **File** and then **Export**.

3 Export the graphic as
HTML and Images.

*Note: See Chapter 13 for more
information on exporting graphics.*

*Note: In the HTML Setup dialog box,
choose **Generic** as the HTML Style
and check **Include HTML
Comments**.*

4 Click **Save**.

5 Open a text editor, such
as Notepad.

6 Open the HTML file.

■ To do so in Notepad, first
click **File** and then **Open**.

■ Click the Look In ▾ and
browse to the folder where
you exported the file.

■ Click the Files of Type ▾
and select **All Files**.

■ Click the name of the
HTML document and then
click **Open**.

What are comments in the HTML file?

Multiline comments begin with `<!--` and end with `-->` in an HTML file. *Comments* consist of notes and advice that you can read, but comments do not show up on the Web page like HTML tags and text do. Comments help you to locate the text to copy, whether for `<table>` tags, `<script>` tags, or other tags. Fireworks and HTML editors add comments to help you locate certain HTML formatting. You can also add comments yourself to your HTML files.

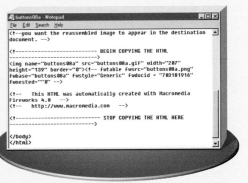

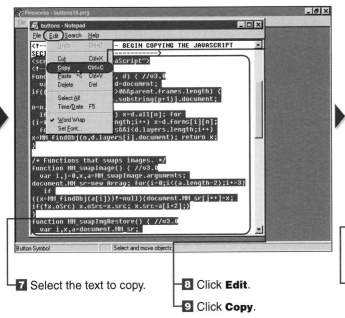

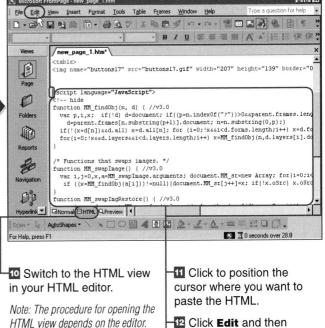

7 Select the text to copy.

8 Click **Edit**.

9 Click **Copy**.

10 Switch to the HTML view in your HTML editor.

*Note: The procedure for opening the HTML view depends on the editor. In FrontPage, you click the **HTML** view tab.*

11 Click to position the cursor where you want to paste the HTML.

12 Click **Edit** and then **Paste**.

■ The JavaScript HTML is pasted into the document.

INDEX

C

canvas, trimming, 274
canvas color, 22
canvas size, 20–21
caret (^) beside the Pen cursor, 61
CCW (counterclockwise), 50
cells, 174–175
Center Alignment button, 45
center-aligned text, attaching to a path, 63
changes, redoing/undoing, 24
checkerboard pattern, 101, 258
circle, drawing, 67, 162, 164
Clipboard, copying HTML code to, 286, 289
Close button, 19
Close command, 32
Color dialog box, 255
color effects, 112–113
color images, changing to grayscale or sepia, 108
Color Mixer command, 72
color palette, 241, 257. *See also* palette
Color Table panel, 252–255
colors
    adding in the Color Table, 255
    adding to the Swatches panel, 73
    applying to fills, 68–69
    changing background, 22
    changing for hotspots, 165
    changing for strokes, 65
    changing for text, 42
    choosing the number of, 257
    creating custom, 14
    deleting from the Color Table, 255
    limiting for graphics, 250
    locating in the Color Table, 253
    locking in the Color Table, 254
    mixing, 72
    picking for objects, 10
    removing selected, 98
    selecting for an animation, 241
    selecting for a pop-up menu, 175
    selecting for text, 43
    setting transparent, 258
    sorting in the Swatches panel, 71
    Web-safe, 70–71
    working with, 70–73

Commands menu, 108–109
comments in an HTML file, 293
compression, effect on graphics, 248
Constrain Proportions check box, 93
contrast, adjusting, 102–103
Convert to Grayscale command, 108
Convert to Sepia Tone command, 109
Convert to Symbol command, 140
Copy command
    in the Edit menu, 47, 142
    on the Object panel, 156
Copy HTML Code dialog box, 286–288
Copy Over Graphic button, 139
Copy to Frames dialog box, 226
CorelDRAW file, opening in Fireworks, 245
Crayon stroke, 65
Creative command, 108–109
Crop Selected Bitmap command, 94
Ctrl key, 14
current instance of a button, 157
curved lines, drawing, 57–59
custom effects, 126–127
cut-out effect, 130
CW (clockwise), 50

D

Default Colors button, 73
default effects, 124–125
default fill, 67, 69
default frame delay, 239
default stroke, 67
defaults, 124
Delete Effect command, 127
Delete Frame command, 225
Delete Layer button, 83
Delete Menu button, 173
depth, 112
disjoint rollover, 199, 214–217
Distort command, 51, 77, 167
Distribute to Frames command, 227
dither, 242
document formats, comparing, 13
document name, 7
document window, 7, 19, 29

INDEX

INDEX

INDEX

Read Less, Learn More™

Visual

Simplified®

Simply the Easiest Way to Learn

For visual learners who are brand-new to a topic and want to be shown, not told, how to solve a problem in a friendly, approachable way.

All *Simplified*® books feature friendly Disk characters who demonstrate and explain the purpose of each task.

Title	ISBN	Price
America Online® Simplified®, 2nd Ed.	0-7645-3433-5	$24.99
Computers Simplified®, 5th Ed.	0-7645-3524-2	$24.99
Creating Web Pages with HTML Simplified®, 2nd Ed.	0-7645-6067-0	$24.99
Excel 97 Simplified®	0-7645-6022-0	$24.99
Excel for Windows® 95 Simpified®	1-56884-682-7	$19.99
FrontPage® 2000 Simplified®	0-7645-3450-5	$24.99
Internet and World Wide Web Simplified®, 3rd Ed.	0-7645-3409-2	$24.99
Lotus® 1-2-3® Release 5 for Windows® Simplified®	1-56884-670-3	$19.99
Microsoft® Access 2000 Simplified®	0-7645-6058-1	$24.99
Microsoft® Excel 2000 Simplified®	0-7645-6053-0	$24.99
Microsoft® Office 2000 Simplified®	0-7645-6052-2	$29.99
Microsoft® Word 2000 Simplified®	0-7645-6054-9	$24.99
More Windows® 95 Simplified®	1-56884-689-4	$19.99
More Windows® 98 Simplified®	0-7645-6037-9	$24.99
Office 97 Simplified®	0-7645-6009-3	$29.99
PC Upgrade and Repair Simplified®	0-7645-6049-2	$24.99
Windows® 95 Simplified®	1-56884-662-2	$19.99
Windows® 98 Simplified®	0-7645-6030-1	$24.99
Windows® 2000 Professional Simplified®	0-7645-3422-X	$24.99
Windows® Me Millennium Edition Simplified®	0-7645-3494-7	$24.99
Word 97 Simplified®	0-7645-6011-5	$24.99

Over 10 million *Visual* books in print!

with these full-color Visual™ guides

The Fast and Easy Way to Learn

 Discover how to use what you learn with "Teach Yourself" tips

Title	ISBN	Price
Teach Yourself Access 97 VISUALLY™	0-7645-6026-3	$29.99
Teach Yourself FrontPage® 2000 VISUALLY™	0-7645-3451-3	$29.99
Teach Yourself HTML VISUALLY™	0-7645-3423-8	$29.99
Teach Yourself the Internet and World Wide Web VISUALLY™, 2nd Ed.	0-7645-3410-6	$29.99
Teach Yourself Microsoft® Access 2000 VISUALLY™	0-7645-6059-X	$29.99
Teach Yourself Microsoft® Excel 97 VISUALLY™	0-7645-6063-8	$29.99
Teach Yourself Microsoft® Excel 2000 VISUALLY™	0-7645-6056-5	$29.99
Teach Yourself Microsoft® Office 2000 VISUALLY™	0-7645-6051-4	$29.99
Teach Yourself Microsoft® PowerPoint® 97 VISUALLY™	0-7645-6062-X	$29.99
Teach Yourself Microsoft® PowerPoint® 2000 VISUALLY™	0-7645-6060-3	$29.99
Teach Yourself More Windows® 98 VISUALLY™	0-7645-6044-1	$29.99
Teach Yourself Netscape Navigator® 4 VISUALLY™	0-7645-6028-X	$29.99
Teach Yourself Office 97 VISUALLY™	0-7645-6018-2	$29.99
Teach Yourself Red Hat® Linux® VISUALLY™	0-7645-3430-0	$29.99
Teach Yourself VISUALLY™ Computers, 3rd Ed.	0-7645-3525-0	$29.99
Teach Yourself VISUALLY™ Dreamweaver® 3	0-7645-3470-X	$29.99
Teach Yourself VISUALLY™ Fireworks® 4	0-7645-3566-8	$29.99
Teach Yourself VISUALLY™ Flash™ 5	0-7645-3540-4	$29.99
Teach Yourself VISUALLY™ iMac™	0-7645-3453-X	$29.99
Teach Yourself VISUALLY™ Investing Online	0-7645-3459-9	$29.99
Teach Yourself VISUALLY™ Networking, 2nd Ed.	0-7645-3534-X	$29.99
Teach Yourself VISUALLY™ Photoshop® 6	0-7645-3513-7	$29.99
Teach Yourself VISUALLY™ Quicken® 2001	0-7645-3526-9	$29.99
Teach Yourself VISUALLY™ Windows® 2000 Server	0-7645-3428-9	$29.99
Teach Yourself VISUALLY™ Windows® Me Millennium Edition	0-7645-3495-5	$29.99
Teach Yourself Windows® 95 VISUALLY™	0-7645-6001-8	$29.99
Teach Yourself Windows® 98 VISUALLY™	0-7645-6025-5	$29.99
Teach Yourself Windows® 2000 Professional VISUALLY™	0-7645-6040-9	$29.99
Teach Yourself Windows NT® 4 VISUALLY™	0-7645-6061-1	$29.99
Teach Yourself Word 97 VISUALLY™	0-7645-6032-8	$29.99

ORDER FORM

TRADE & INDIVIDUAL ORDERS

Phone: **(800) 762-2974**
or **(317) 572-3993**
(8 a.m.–6 p.m., CST, weekdays)
FAX : **(800) 550-2747**
or **(317) 572-4002**

EDUCATIONAL ORDERS & DISCOUNTS

Phone: **(800) 434-2086**
(8:30 a.m.–5:00 p.m., CST, weekdays)
FAX : **(317) 572-4005**

CORPORATE ORDERS FOR VISUAL™ SERIES

Phone: **(800) 469-6616**
(8 a.m.–5 p.m., EST, weekdays)
FAX : **(905) 890-9434**

Qty	ISBN	Title	Price	Total

Shipping & Handling Charges

	Description	First book	Each add'l. book	Total
Domestic	Normal	$4.50	$1.50	$
	Two Day Air	$8.50	$2.50	$
	Overnight	$18.00	$3.00	$
International	Surface	$8.00	$8.00	$
	Airmail	$16.00	$16.00	$
	DHL Air	$17.00	$17.00	$

Subtotal _____

CA residents add
applicable sales tax _____

IN, MA and MD
residents add
5% sales tax _____

IL residents add
6.25% sales tax _____

RI residents add
7% sales tax _____

TX residents add
8.25% sales tax _____

Shipping _____

Total _____

Ship to:

Name_____

Address_____

Company_____

City/State/Zip_____

Daytime Phone_____

Payment: ☐ Check to Hungry Minds (US Funds Only)
☐ Visa   ☐ Mastercard   ☐ American Express

Card # _____ Exp. _____ Signature_____